INSTANT SALES

Other Books in the Instant Success Series

Successful Franchising by Bradley J. Sugars
The Real Estate Coach by Bradley J. Sugars
Billionaire in Training by Bradley J. Sugars
Instant Cashflow by Bradley J. Sugars
Instant Leads by Bradley J. Sugars
Instant Profit by Bradley J. Sugars
Instant Promotions by Bradley J. Sugars
Instant Repeat Business by Bradley J. Sugars
Instant Team Building by Bradley J. Sugars
Instant Systems by Bradley J. Sugars
Instant Referrals by Bradley J. Sugars
Instant Advertising by Bradley J. Sugars
The Business Coach by Bradley J. Sugars

INSTANT SALES

BRADLEY J. SUGARS

McGraw-Hill

New York   Chicago   San Francisco   Lisbon   London
Madrid   Mexico City   Milan   New Delhi   San Juan
Seoul   Singapore   Sydney   Toronto

4 5 6 7 8 9 0   FGR/FGR   0 9 8

ISBN 0-07-146664-9

This publication is designed to provide accurate and authoritative information in regard to the subject matter covered. It is sold with the understanding that neither the author nor the publisher is engaged in rendering legal, accounting, or other professional service. If legal advice or other expert assistance is required, the services of a competent professional person should be sought.
—From a Declaration of Principles jointly adopted by Committee of the American Bar Association and a Committee of Publishers.

McGraw-Hill books are available at special quantity discounts to use as premiums and sales promotions, or for use in corporate training programs. For more information, please write to the Director of Special Sales, McGraw-Hill Professional, Two Penn Plaza, New York, NY 10121-2298. Or contact your local bookstore.

Library of Congress Cataloging-in-Publication Data

Sugars, Bradley J.
Instant sales / Bradley J. Sugars.
p. cm.
ISBN 0-07-146664-9 (alk. paper)
1. Selling.   I. Title.
HF438. 25.S835 2006
658.85—dc22   2005025420

To all Action Business Coaches,
leaders in every sense of the word.

■ CONTENTS

▌ Introduction

So you've got your prospect right there in front of you. How do you make the sale? Let me put it this way. How do you convert the prospect into a customer?

That's the million-dollar question that has eluded so many sales people over the years. Yet it needn't be. You see, selling is simple, as long as you follow the rules of the game.

By reading this book, you'll discover the secrets of selling. You'll also discover that the sales process actually starts well before you get to the stage of meeting your prospect face-to-face. You may even be surprised to discover this process actually starts with *you*.

In this book, I'm going to show you how to maximize your Conversion Rate, or to put it another way, how to make sure your prospects actually buy from you. But I'm also going to explain some not-so-well-known techniques that are aimed at smoothing your path through the sales process. These techniques are designed to give you every chance of consummating the sale long before you get face-to-face with your prospect. These include topics such as how to win more business through giving great quotes, how to write killer scripts for telephone inquiries that get fantastic results, and how to produce a Point of Sale system to generate increased sales for your business.

With this in mind, where does the sales process fit in the overall scheme of business? To give you a better idea, I'm going to briefly mention a very important concept. This is the concept I call The Business Chassis. Read more about this in my book *Instant Cashflow*.

The Business Chassis looks like this: (See the following chart)

LEADS
(prospects or potential customers)

X

CONVERSION RATE
(the difference between those that could have bought and those that did)

=

CUSTOMERS
(the number of different customers you deal with)

X

NUMBER OF TRANSACTIONS
(the average number of times each customer bought from you that year)

X

AVERAGE DOLLAR SALE PRICE
(the average price of the items you sell)

=

TOTAL REVENUE
(the total turnover of the business)

X

MARGINS
(the percentage of each sale that's profit)

=

PROFIT
(something every business owner wants more of)

As you can see, sales have to do with the first three parts of the Business Chassis. The process begins when you decide to generate leads (read my books *Instant Leads* and *Instant Promotions* for more in-depth information about this) and end up with some prospects—or people who were interested enough to respond to your lead generation efforts. They will typically make themselves known at this stage. Your task then is to convert them from being just prospects to becoming customers.

So, congratulations on deciding to take proactive steps to growing your business. By concentrating on first things first, you'll set in motion a chain of activities that will generate more company for your business by increasing your conversion rate. I personally guarantee it.

This book is designed to give you the inside track on everything you need to know about how to convert prospects into customers. It aims at providing you with an *instant* guide on how to overcome objections, build rapport, communicate, and be professional. Once you've read this book, you'll know precisely what it takes to sell successfully.

This book is the next step in your marketing success story. From this moment on, you won't have to dream about the day when you're recognized as a leader in your field. You'll know precisely what to do to make it a reality. You'll also know exactly how to go about increasing your conversion rate.

▌ How to Use This Book

This book is divided into different parts, one for each of the major areas I'll be discussing.

Pick the part that interests you most, jump right in, and begin working through the steps outlined. You see, there are things you must give careful consideration to before getting carried away doing the "fun" things involved in selling.

You'll notice repetition in many of the steps outlined. This is because this book outlines, in practical terms, how to go about improving the way you sell. Much of it is based on the fundamental steps in the selling process. These steps largely involve the same core functions or techniques, with improvements or enhancements added to suit the situation.

You might decide to implement all the great ideas explained in this book all at once. Or you might decide to implement them one at a time. But whatever you decide, the important thing is, you'll no longer be blundering around in the dark, unsure whether what you're doing has a chance of bringing in more business or not.

In this book you'll meet my mechanic, Charlie. He's a great guy and he's looked after my cars for years. But as a businessman—well, he's a great mechanic. Fortunately he's also a realist, and when he realized his business could be doing a whole lot better, he approached me and asked for help. Follow his case and learn more about sales as you do so.

You might also be surprised at how much this exercise will reveal about your business. It may get you thinking about important issues that have never crossed your mind before. If some of this information is new to you, don't be concerned—there's never been a better time to start improving the way you sell.

Make sure you take notes as you go along. When you come to deciding what you're going to do to improve your bottom line, you'll find it useful referring back to them. You'll find proven examples and ideas that, when combined with your new knowledge, will bring results.

Now it's time to get started. There are customers out there waiting to deal with you.

■ Charlie Concentrates on Conversion Rate

"Hey, Charlie," I said, climbing out of my new car. "What do you think about this little beauty?"

"Wow, Brad, that's some car you've got there. When did you buy it?"

"Yesterday. You're the first to see it, Charlie. Just wait till you see what's under the hood!"

I could see he was itching to have a look, so I popped the hood and watched as his eyes lit up.

"Man, that's some power plant you've got there. Just look at those extractors! What's its output?"

"You're not going to believe this—500 horses in the old language. How good is that?"

"Get out of here . . . no, on second thought, you'd better come in before we get carried away."

Charlie and I had always loved talking cars ever since he first worked on mine. He was a fantastic mechanic, but sadly, his business skills weren't on a par. That's typical of most small business owners, I thought. It's a symptom of one of the most common mistakes people make when starting a small business. They tend to get involved with what they know best. You know, a hairdresser opens up a salon, a baker opens a bakery, and a mechanic opens a workshop. Big mistake. See, they end up *doing* the work, working *in* the business instead of *on* it. Charlie was no different.

Well, in one sense he was; he recognized his shortcoming and called me in to help.

"Today we're going to look at selling, Charlie. You see, this is one area that is vital to any business. You've got to be able to *sell* to people to stay in business. Putting it another way, you've got to be able to *convert* your prospects into customers."

"Yeah, I'm with you Brad. But I'm just not the sales type, if you know what I mean. I'm not one of those flashy guys with the gift of the gab."

Another common misconception, I thought to myself.

"Sales is a far more comprehensive subject than that, Charlie. You see, what we're essentially dealing with when I say 'selling' or 'sales' is everything involved in the process of converting prospects into customers. This involves things like providing written guarantees, being able to define your uniqueness, stocking an exclusive line, packaging, having a toll-free number, accepting trade-ins, providing tours of your site, and a whole lot more. In fact, we use a tried-and-tested list of over 80 different tools to help convert prospects into customers."

"I had no idea, man. No wonder my business has been rather unpredictable."

"That's what I'm going to show you how to fix. You see, as long as you're realistic, methodical, and committed to succeeding, there's no reason on earth why you shouldn't be able to turn your business around."

Charlie was becoming a good student.

"OK, Charlie, before we get down to the nitty gritty, do you have any idea what your current conversion rate is?"

"What exactly do you mean by that, Brad?"

"It's the percentage of people who did business with you as compared to those who could have. For example, if you had 10 people walk through your door today and you sold to only 3 of them, you'd have a conversion rate of 3 out of 10, or 30 percent. This has got to be a literal goldmine. You see, you've already got them interested; now you've just got to get them over the line."

"I'm quite good in this area, I reckon, Brad. I'd say once people come in and I get talking to them, they'll almost certainly bring their cars in. But to put a figure on it? I'm not sure."

"You're not alone here, Charlie. When I ask the average business owners about their conversion rate, most take a stab in the dark and tell me it's between 60 and 70 percent. Just for fun, I get them to measure it, and a couple of weeks later we find it's more like 20 or 30 percent. Imagine how they feel."

I could tell he was able to relate to this as he was frowning now and looking at his hands on his lap.

"You should feel great if that were you," I continued. "In fact you should be excited, because if you're getting by at 20 or 30 percent, imagine how your business would run at 60 or 70 percent. Remember, double your conversion rate and you've just doubled your revenue."

"That's incredible, Brad. You're making me excited already."

"Good. Now listen up. Here's what we'll be discussing today. In a moment, I'm going to go over everything you need to know about selling in general. I'm going to make sales simple for you. Then we'll discuss quotes and how you can use them to convert more prospects. We're going to look at scripts. That's right, you need a good script to take care of things like handling objections and queries. Then we'll take a good, hard look at customer service. I'll show you how to make your business fire on all cylinders by turning your prospects not only into customers, but into Raving Fans. Then we'll concentrate on the telephone and how you can use it to your advantage. And finally, I'll show you all you need to know about Point of Sale and how you can make money in ways you've never thought about. How does that sound, Charlie?"

"Fantastic, Brad. Can't wait to start."

INSTANT SALES

Part 1

■ Sales Made Simple

What Is Selling?

"To really get to understand how you can dramatically improve your selling skills, Charlie, it's necessary to first understand what selling is. Well, I know you already know that, but let me tell you the way I see it. Let me give you my definition of selling."

"OK, Brad, I'm curious. I'll bet it's not what I expect. I'll bet it's not something along the lines of being able to convince someone to buy what it is you're selling."

"You're nearly there, Charlie. Listen to what I say it is, and note where the emphasis falls. Selling is nothing more than *professionally* helping other people to buy. Get it?"

I could see he was a little surprised.

"The key word here is 'professionally.' Yet how many professional salespeople know how to sell? They may think they know, but do they really? How good are they? To answer this question, we really need to know a little bit more about the individual salesperson."

"But that's ridiculous, Brad. How can we know anything about a salesperson? How could we possibly know about every single salesperson out there?"

"The answer to that, Charlie, is to analyze the different types of salespeople. That's a lot easier because they all, in some way or another, fall into one of the following four basic groups:

- The Order Taker.
    This person waits for people to ask if they can buy.

- The Product Pusher.
    This person talks about nothing more than the product.

1

- The Problem Solver.
    This person helps the customers find what they need.

- The Over Seller
    This person promises the world just to get a sale.

"Are you with me?"

"Yeah. I follow what you're saying. I'd never thought of it that way. But tell me about these different types—I'm intrigued."

The Characteristics of a Good Salesperson

There's another characteristic professional salespeople have in common: they train. They train continuously. And they keep training. They do this for a number of very good reasons. First, they want to keep up-to-date with the latest trends and techniques. And in today's fast-changing world, this can be a bit of a challenge. Second, they want to keep motivated. They want their energy levels replenished on a regular basis. One of the best ways of doing this is to rub shoulders with successful salespeople on a regular basis. You see, one of the powerful benefits of doing this is to hear from them what works and what doesn't. It also helps keep them focused on the bigger picture, on what is achievable, and on how they can lift their game by emulating the best in the business.

To be successful in sales, you need to have strong beliefs. You need to have something you believe to be true. But more particularly, you need to hold a strong set of beliefs about salespeople in general (and you in particular), about your customers, and about the product or service you sell.

You need to understand that, when customers are making up their minds whether to buy or not, those decisions will be based on a mixture of fact and emotion. This is due to our human nature. We can't get away from it. But the important thing you need to know, when faced with a customer in this situation, is what percentage of the decision will be based on fact, and what percentage on emotion. If you knew that, you'd be in a far better position to help with the process. Of course, this varies according to the type of product being considered, but on average, the decision is a mix of 20 percent logic and 80 percent emotion. How powerful is this to know?

To be successful at selling, you also need to hold strong beliefs about money. What does it mean to you and what role does it play as a motivator? It's pretty important to most salespeople, because their very remuneration package usually hinges on their performance. The more successful they are at selling, the more they earn. It's as simple as that.

Money seems to feature prominently in the life of a salesperson. And so it should. But what is money?

Let me give you my view.

Money is an idea backed by confidence.

Different, huh? That's right. To succeed out there, you need to see things differently. If you don't, you'll be no different from the rest. Understand this: If you see things just as every one else does, you'll get the same results as they do. And we all know most salespeople don't make a fabulous living.

So let me run this past you once more. Money is an idea backed by confidence. This is where I get back to what I mentioned at the beginning of this book. Remember when I said the sales process starts with *you?* Long before you have a prospect to convert, and long before you are at the stage of selling a product to a prospect, you only have an idea. You have the idea that you'd like to sell this or that to someone. Of course, you have this idea because it's what you do for a living. You need the income to get by each and every month. But you don't only have an idea. You have something more. You have confidence. That's right. Because you are a professional salesperson, you have confidence in your ability to sell. At this stage, you might not know who you will be selling to, or precisely what, but you'll probably have a vague idea. For instance, if you sell real estate, you probably know you'll be selling some house to someone during the course of the week or month. Just who to and which one might not be known, but you will be confident of achieving that before the month is out. Now, when you combine the idea with the confidence, the end result is money. The money will follow. Get it?

Now if you see money as I do, the way you set out to get it is by harnessing the power of the following four words: Attention, Interest, Desire, and Action.

You need to focus your attention on your goals. You then need to have a strong interest in achieving these goals. Mix this with a strong desire to achieve, and you'll be spurred into *Action*. You'll rise to the occasion and perform.

Every salesperson needs to be a good communicator to succeed. Communication is the lifeblood of business, and when it comes to sales, it's vital. It has a direct relationship with sales. You see, the better you are at communicating, the better your sales results will be. You can almost measure the one with the other. Actually one could be thought of as a barometer for the other. Let me put it another way. True communication is the response you get. So if you're not getting the response you want, you're not communicating properly.

Let's look at this in more detail. Communication, as far as sales is concerned, isn't confined to the words alone. It's far broader than that. In fact, when it comes to communicating, the salesperson has three tools at his disposal: words, voice, and body language. And we use them all simultaneously. The interesting thing, as far as communication in the sales process is concerned, is that words account for only 7 percent of the eventual outcome, the voice is more significant at 38 percent, but by far the most important tool is body language, which weighs in at 55 percent.

Have a good look at these figures.

Remember what I said about your ideas and your confidence? Understand how they influence your body language, and you'll begin to grasp the importance of this in the sales process.

Neuro-Linguistic Programming

I'm now going to introduce another concept that has to do with communication in the broad sense. It's called Neuro-Linguistic Programming, or NLP for short. NLP is a model of human behavior and communication that draws from the knowledge of psychodynamics and behavioral theories. It is concerned with the identification of both conscious and unconscious patterns in communication and behavior and how they interact in the process of change.

So what does this mean as far as sales are concerned?

If we can understand the three key components of NLP, we can become better communicators. These are:

- Rapport and communication.
- Gathering information.
- Change strategies and interventions.

4

Rapport and communication covers areas such as language, representational systems, eye-accessing movements, verbal and nonverbal pacing and leading, communication translation skills, and representational system overlapping.

Understanding NLP allows us to understand the processes people use to encode and transfer their experience and to guide and modify their behavior. All the information gathering is done through three sensory systems: the visual, the auditory, and kinesthetic (feeling and touching). And to a lesser extent, we also use our senses of smell and taste, but these are not of any significance. The really interesting thing here is that visual accounts for 40 percent of the way we communicate, auditory only 20 percent, and kinesthetic 40 percent. Isn't that interesting?

So, what does this mean for the salesperson? Well, one of the big lessons here is to learn to match the language system used by your prospects. That way you build rapport very quickly. But be careful not to mimic their language—rather match and mirror the way they communicate.

Successful salespeople also understand the various behavioral styles people have. They understand that people fall into one of four main behavioral groups. They can be either outgoing in nature or reserved. Or they can be either task oriented or people oriented.

The DISC Personality Profile

It would help if we were able to understand, in broad terms, the way people behave. Understanding this would make our lives much easier when it comes to interacting with them and assisting them to make purchasing decisions.

One system I recommend is the DISC Personality Profile. The American psychologist Dr. William Moulton Marsden designed this system back in the 1920s. It places people into one of four different personality types, or categories: D—Dominant, I—Influential, S—Steady, and C—Compliant.

The DISC Personality Profile is an accurate personality analysis that can be used to predict the behavior of individuals when they work on their own and with others. However, this system is not infallible. Like anything, it has its limitations. Its shortfall is that people seldom have just one personality. They are, rather, a combination of the four, just in different ratios. Everyone is dominant in one personality type, but another may be closely following.

The DISC test highlights a person's relative strengths in each of the four areas. The area that scores highest will be the person's dominant trait.

The results aren't always accurate, especially when the people being tested are aware of their personality eccentricities and have moved to improve these traits. The higher the strength shown from the test, the more the descriptions will fit. Don't use this as a definitive method for labeling people's traits. Use it as a guide to communicating with them.

Everyone has weaknesses, and this system is meant as a guide to them. Remember, if you are happy as you are, that's great.

When you read the characteristics of the various personality types, you will start to understand how other people see you when they associate with you. Again, this isn't always true. With all knowledge should come wisdom. Knowing the best time and way to use this knowledge is what makes the difference.

People under Pressure

To better understand this section, remember the four main personality types: D—Dominant, I—Influential, S—Steady and, C—Compliant.

People can change their nature under pressure. A High I can become a High S under pressure. This means the person slows down and thinks more; he becomes more reserved.

A High I can become a High D, which means instead of being friendly to everyone, she starts to boss everyone around without much regard for their feelings. People around her would wonder what happened to that friendly person who got on with everyone so well.

A High D can become a High C under pressure. She will now consider details more and think carefully before making a decision. A High D could go to a High S, meaning she will steady herself and slow down. She will consider the people around her more.

A High S could even become a High D under pressure. He now has to act and think quickly when placed under lots of pressure. He might start to become loud and bark out orders when normally he is calm, reserved, and friendly.

A High C could move to a High D under pressure. She will think and act more quickly than previously, making decisions quickly and not consider all the details. You've heard people say that they work best under pressure; this could mean they've become a High D under pressure to get more done.

Normally a High C wouldn't change to a High I or High S under pressure, or a High I wouldn't go to a High C under pressure, as these two personality types are so different.

Often a person stays the same under pressure. A High D can stay a High D. A High S can stay a High S, and so on. Not everyone changes under pressure. You will know when someone does. It will be quite noticeable.

High I Personalities

High I's like to have fun and be popular. You can recognize them by their outgoing and very friendly manner. They want to be people's friends. They will rarely tell anyone off. When they say something in anger, they don't want you to remind them of it again because that was in the past and they really weren't that serious when they said it in the first place.

High I's don't like to get into too much detail, as they don't find that fun. They like to work with others in a changing environment. High I's can be recognized by their very friendly disposition. They look you in the eye and usually use a lot of tonal changes in their voice.

They talk a bit louder than other personality types, except the High D who can also talk confidently and loudly. This is the mark of an extrovert. The difference between them is that High I's are loud and friendly. If you joke with either of them, a High I will respond but a High D may not.

High I's will respond quicker because they think you're like them, so they'll let you know by giving you a friendly response.

High I Interaction

High I's get on fairly well with most personality types. They can annoy the High C and High D because they're task-oriented and just want to get the job done without being friendly while doing it. All the other personality types can see a

High I as overly friendly. They might say, "Mellow out a bit. You come on too strong and annoy people. Don't be so friendly."

High I's are good motivators and team leaders, although they won't like pulling team members into line if they've done something they shouldn't have.

Selling to a High I

To sell to High I's you need to win them over and be their friend. If you don't show you care about them or that you like them, they won't want to buy from you.

You need to show you have a sense of humor, are a fun-loving person, and you are having fun talking to them right now. You can work on being a little bit stern but not too serious.

High I's want to do what seems popular. They don't want to do anything that seems like detailed work that will take up lots of their time. If it seems boring to them, they won't want it. The best thing you can say to them is it will be a lot of fun.

They will buy from people who seem to have the same nature as they do. So be happy and spontaneous. Talk about other things apart from what you are selling them. Get chatty at the start, during the middle, and the end of the selling process. They will sometimes want to go off on a tangent. Let them do most of the talking. They love to talk about anything, especially other people.

Be their friend and advise them on what you think and feel is best for them. Be sincere. Be like them and they will love you.

If you're a High D, don't talk too much. Let them decide they want it and that it seems like a popular idea and makes sense. High D's need to be friendlier than they usually are when being sold to.

You can't be too friendly with High I's—as long as you're sincere. They are people persons and have great people skills. They won't like you if you are fake.

High I's are prone to exaggerate. They like to tell stories, and you can too when selling to them. But tell them if you are exaggerating.

Areas They Need to Work On

High I's need to work on getting the job done and not being distracted by other people. They need to be more task oriented. They need to get into the details more, as this is what they don't like doing.

They need to be less extroverted with people, especially High C's and High S's. When communicating with High C's they don't need to be their friend, which is what they believe.

High I's are a bit too friendly for the High S, although High S's can see that aspect of them and not let it bother them. High I's need to recognize that the other personality types are not like them. They also need to work on being more like the others when communicating with them.

High D Personalities

High D's like to be in control. They want to be at the top and give the orders. They have a hard time following orders, as they feel their own way is always better. High D's will usually end up in management positions, self-employed, or in charge of a section that has a bit of room to move unsupervised.

They like to be in control of their own lives and make their own decisions. High D's can seem to be too powerful or too strong for other people. They are confident, outspoken, and say what they feel. This can offend others, as they can be thought of as arrogant. They aren't usually; it's just the way that they express themselves.

As High D's have active minds that like to be stimulated, they like to be doing lots of things at once. When they do more than one thing at a time, the quality can start to drop. It can be difficult for them to follow something to its end. They feel a great need for lots of activity. When you want something done in a hurry, give it to a High D.

High D Interaction

High D's do not interact well with others. They give orders and like to take control and this can detract from their relationships with others.

High D's can sabotage or undermine the authority of a High I and not be at all worried about it affecting their popularity. While the High I likes to have fun working with a group, the High D isn't that interested, or at least not to the same degree.

Often High D's have a lot of High I in them; they just need to tap into it a bit more to get on better with a High I.

High D's work well with High C's. Neither needs to be friendly while they work, so they get the job done. The two personalities compliment each other very well. The High D gets on best with a High C. A High D likes to delegate, and the best one to delegate to is the High C.

However, because the High D is not detail-oriented and the High C is, a problem can occur. The High C will need lots of details on how to do something, and this is precisely something the High D doesn't like to give.

Also, High C's prefer to do the same thing over and over. They like doing what they know how to do. That's often how they get their significance and feelings of importance, by doing something perfectly.

A High D gets along reasonably well with a High S because the latter is steadying, reserved, and tolerant of others. High S's don't need to be given the details like a High C does. They can just be told what to do and they do it.

High S's know that High D's likes to control others and don't let it worry them. High D's don't consider their mode of interaction, like needing to relay instructions with details for the High C, or with friendliness to a High I, so the High S works best with a High D.

High D's may think High S's are inferior because they mistake their natural reserve and steadiness with lacking in confidence. Often High S's have great self-confidence; they just don't need to display it like a High D does. High D's like confident people, as they can relate better to them.

Selling to a High D

High D's like to be leaders. They like to do what no one else is doing. They like to be innovative pioneers. The best way to sell to them is to tell them that they need to be more productive, profitable, successful, and leaders of others.

Respect them and never make them feel inferior. They need to respect the sales person. Most importantly, they need to be confident you can deliver what you say you can. They need to be given the facts and reasons. Also don't try and be too friendly with them.

They want a summary of any features. They don't need details; in fact, going over details annoys them. Give a brief outline of different things showing the logic of it all. They want to be productive, so tell them what you have will help that cause. Tell them that they will be more successful using your service or item. That's what they want to know.

Give them better solutions or ways of doing things. Be blunt if you have to; they don't mind too much and they don't care—but only if they have your respect.

Areas They Need to Work On

The major area they need to work on is their people skills and communication with others. They also need to slow down to check if they are making progress. When talking to High C's, they need to give more specifics.

They need to be friendlier to others they work with. They need to have a checking system on their progress and of how well they are doing. Are the jobs they start being completed, and if so, how good is the quality? They need to stop, plan, and think more before they start, and also as they progress.

High S Personalities

High S's are steady people. They don't like to rush things. When everyone else is stressing out, they remain calm. They like to plod along, thinking things over before doing anything. They don't like making quick decisions.

They are well liked by all personality types because they are friendly, easy-going, and harmless. People admire their cool disposition. They just get in and get the job done, although usually not at a great pace.

While the High D's start, going flat out without knowing if they are doing it right, the High I's get everyone together so they can all get involved and have fun.

The High C plans every detail meticulously before making a start, while the High S thinks it over for a fair while before making a slow start.

High S Interaction

High S's get on well with High D's because they probably understand them, and it doesn't worry them when the High D gives orders. Because the High S's are calm, they are a help to the High D.

High S's can plan things, which is a help to the High D. They slow the High D down, and this can be both a good thing and a bad. High D's often end up marrying High S's.

The High S gets along well with the High I. They are both people oriented. The High S is a calmer, more reserved version of the High I. The High S might say to the High I, "Mellow out. You come on too strong. You're too friendly." While the High I will respond, "Get a bit more life in you."

They both have fun in life, or try to. The High S has a high concern for others and tries to understand them. When High I's work with High S's, they can often get carried away with having fun, as they're not as task-oriented as the High D and High C.

The two usually won't get as much done as the other two personality types.

High S and High C are both introverted. They both like to take their time in making a decision. They work well together, although they won't get a task done as quickly as the D's and I's. They will think about it for a while first.

The High S will feel there's no need to rush into it. High C's will agree because they will want to consider all the details before they start anyway. The High C's will be planning it out perfectly before they start, and if it's taking too long to start, the High S's won't say too much because they like to keep the peace.

However, the two personality types will get a job done well together and it will be done correctly.

The High D and High S get a job done well and compliment each other nicely. The High S will bring the High D's feet back down to earth and steady them. The High D will speed up the High S's decision-making process, which is sometimes needed.

The High S admires the High D's leadership ability, while the High D admires the High S's steadiness—although not always. Because the High S is reserved while the High D is outgoing, they learn from each other in different situations.

Selling to a High S

They are harder to sell to than the High D or I. They like to be steady in their decision making. They don't like to rush anything. They like to take their time in reaching a decision. They don't like pressure or pushy people.

You need to be their friend and build genuine rapport with them. Be reserved like they are. Be casual. Outline what you want them to buy, and then give details. Give them data to make a decision and tell them they need to make it soon.

Don't expect quick decisions, though. Explain at the start that if you can give them everything they want and expect today, and you both agree it's the best thing, then you'll outline the steps needed to get the process under way. Then ask if it's OK to do that. Get them to commit to making a decision then and there if you can.

Sometimes High S's won't make a decision at all on the day. If that's the case, be aware that it often happens. Give them some time and get back to them the next day. Be firm in wanting a decision soon (or today) but don't be pushy.

Be reserved like they are. High S's don't like change, so tell them your product won't involve any major changes. Tell them it's a nice, slow process.

Give them plenty of eye contact. Build rapport and be their friend.

Areas They Need to Work On

High S's need to work on changing their ways more quickly. They change in time; however, they are the most reluctant of all personality types to do so. High D's will change before you finish telling them why they need to. To High I's change is fun. They like change because they like variety in their life.

High C's won't usually change much at all. This is because they have just finished learning how to do something the best way they can and now they just want to keep doing it. They love getting into a routine and staying that way. How can you achieve perfection in anything if you don't stick to it for ages?

High S's need to practice making quick decisions and not looking back once they've made the decision. They need to realize that often a quick decision is better than no decision at all.

High C Personalities

The High C's are interesting in many ways. They have a tendency to collect data, facts, and figures. They can often stutter their words when describing things, possibly due to tension and also because they are thinking what the perfect way to describe this is. High C's often stutter more than other personality types.

High C's like to do things very well, if not perfectly. However, they don't reference their standards to others, which would be valuable to them because then they would learn that their standards are much higher than everyone else's.

They often create stress in their lives by this ongoing striving to live up to their own perfect standards. They can miss out on seeing the big picture, as they can get stuck on the details.

They want to work on their own because they feel they will do the job best. They think other people won't do as good a job as they will. High C's are reserved and task oriented, which means they aren't that friendly in communication with other people, especially nonfamily and friends.

They like to give lots of data when they communicate, as they feel this is what people want.

They can have high levels of stress due to rarely being able to live up to their own high standards. They like to have many details before making a decision. They virtually never rush into anything, especially without considering all the facts, data, and graphs. Then they like to think about it more.

They don't like to be pushed into doing things, as they feel their way is nearly always the best. They like to plan things out before lifting a finger. Conditions usually have to be perfect before they proceed.

High C Interaction

A High C complements a High D because they are virtual opposites; one is introverted and the other is extroverted. The High C is reserved while the High D is outgoing. Both are task oriented.

High C's get self-satisfaction and pride from doing things for others. Although if they don't know how to do what the High D is asking, there can be problems.

The High C needs to be shown in detail how to do something. The High D isn't into details, so a communication problem can occur. For this pairing to work, the High D's need to explain in more detail how to do the things they want done.

A High C and High I are an interesting combination. They can work well together, although they can often have troubles. When they struggle in relationships, it can be due to their opposite natures. A High I is extroverted, while a High C is introverted.

A High I person is people-oriented while a High C is task-oriented. These traits can cause a lot of conflict. The High I will say or think that the High C is spending too much time on unimportant things. The High C may think the High I is flaky and doesn't work on what is really important.

The High C will want the High I to be less friendly and more task oriented, while the High I will think the opposite.

As a working combination, the two are good for each other if they can put aside their differences. High I's will stop the High C's from being introverted and get them to have more fun and work with others. High C's will bring the High I's back down to earth and get them working on the details. As a combination in business, they can work well together.

Selling to a High C

Selling to a High C can be challenging. High C's can be very skeptical of anyone who says they have something they'll need, because they often feel what they already have is good.

They can often resist change because they have their own way of doing things. They won't consider making a buying decision unless the facts are shown, are valid, and there are lots of them.

Be prepared to spend a lot of time with them. They will ask a hundred questions and procrastinate because they will be wondering whether they've covered every detail they need to know about.

They will be wary of sales people. This is mainly because they have found how to do things without anyone's help, and a new system will mean they'll need to relearn. They're much happier doing what they already know how to do.

They aren't overly friendly like the High I and High S. You can't just tell them they need your item like you can the High D. They only want one thing: data. So give them as much data as you can. And give it in graph form, table from, written form, or essay from.

You can't give High C's too much data to consider. They like to justify their decisions by logic. They don't care if you are their best friend—they always consider the facts first.

Don't expect High C's to make quick decisions. They like time to think. So give it to them. Talk about facts backed up by logic. Get back to them another day, only if you tell them you've given them everything they need to make a decision.

They are confident in their own abilities and are used to relying on making their own decisions. They will talk confidently because they have a lot of knowledge and are proud of it. If you tell them you have a way of helping them do things better and more efficiently, you will get their attention, and possibly the sale, eventually. Anything that improves their standards or efficiency they will love. Tell them they'll be able to do even better with this.

Areas They Need to Work On

Their own standards can be too high compared to others. They can be stressed people due to their feeling that everything they do needs to be perfect. This is the standard they always strive for. It can come from the fact they don't realize their standards are already far above anyone else's.

They need to get other people's opinions when working on a task and accept their standards as being good enough. A High C needs to strive for excellence, not perfection!

Most High C's think they can do a better job, and often they can. But usually the standard a High C works to is the minority's opinion because everyone else acknowledges excellence while a High C keeps on chasing perfection. High C's need to stop at excellence.

They need to work more with others to get used to their level of excellence, and then to accept it as their own "new" standard.

High C's need to be more confident in their approach to decision making and not fear arriving at a wrong decision. After all, High D's make decisions a lot more quickly than a High C ever will. High D's far, far, outweigh High C's when it comes to successful people. So High C's need to get into the habit of making quicker decisions so they can develop a better, stronger, emotional muscle.

High C's need to do things that are new or different. They need to forget their schedule. Throw it away for a day. Do something on the spur of the moment. Do something because it looks like fun. They need to tell themselves that change is fun, that it is good. They need to be more spontaneous.

They also need to get more help from others. They need to ask themselves if what they are doing is the most important thing they could be doing. Will spending the time doing it perfectly really benefit them or others, or should they say, "This is excellent. What can I do next?"

High C's need to move on more. They need to get more involved with people. They need to open up and tell others what they are feeling. A very wise man once said, "Vulnerability is strength because you open yourself up to change and improvement."

High C's need to be spontaneous more often. They need to take on more like a High D does. They need to do more things at once so they don't get stuck on the details that aren't always important.

Purpose

Great salespeople have a purpose. Ever noticed that? It's true. Focus on your prospect and you'll always come out in front.

Do you have a purpose? Or have you never really thought about it? Have you always just assumed you have a purpose—something like needing to sell to meet your sales quotas or commission targets?

Sit down now and write your own Purpose Statement. That's right—get it down on paper. Be careful not to confuse your goals with your purpose. Your goals are the more immediate things you are aiming for, like hitting a certain sales target, earning a certain amount in commission each month, or converting a certain number of prospects into customers each week. Your purpose is more long term. It touches on the very fundamentals of your existence, on what you want out of life in the broad sense. A purpose could be, for instance, to help people feel good about themselves. You see, such a purpose would involve the notion of caring for others—for your customers. It shifts the attention away from what *you* want to what *your customers* want.

Once you have a purpose, start selling on purpose. That's right. Sell on purpose and not by accident, and sell according to the principles of your purpose. Selling according to a fundamental purpose, like the one I've just mentioned, means you'll need to revisit your selling technique. Develop a process that ensures you sell according to the basic fundamentals of your purpose. Here's what I mean:

- Get your prospect's permission before you begin the selling process.
- Begin your selling process by making sure to include lots of questions.
- Offer solutions to your prospect's problems.
- Seek your prospect's agreement before pushing for a decision.
- Explain the investment they are making by purchasing.
- Include a strong call to *Action*.
- Ask permission to finalize the sale.

The Questioning Process

A problem solver's best weapon is the humble question. Not only does this help you in finding out exactly what your customers want, it's a great way to build rapport. It's also a surefire way of having your prospect do the selling for you. You see, by working your way through a structured, and logical, sequence of questions, you'll find that your prospects overcome all the hurdles standing in the way of their decision to buy.

We all, as buyers, go through the same process whereby we investigate various options, eliminating the unsuitable as we go. What we are actually looking for during our encounters with salespeople are reasons why we *shouldn't* buy that particular product then and there. That's part of the "shopping around" process. Your job, as a salesperson, is to help the buyers realize (or decide) your product or service is the one for them. But if it isn't, you need to suggest an alternative. You'll only know this by asking them a series of questions. This allows you to hone in on exactly what it is they're after.

Remember, ask lots of open-ended questions. They're the ones that start with *who, what, where, when, why,* or *how.* Also be specific. Focus on the solution to their problem, and test their "temperature" frequently to see if they are getting warmer or colder. Provide detailed answers. One of my Golden Rules to the art of asking great questions is to play dumb and dig deep. Even if you know a lot about your subject, pretend you don't. Ask the obvious and show an interest in your prospect. It will assist them in opening up on an emotional level. And remember, it's on this level that most purchasing decisions will be made.

Ask question softeners. These begin with the following:

"Can I just ask. . .?"

"By the way. . .?"

"Incidentally. . .?"

They're a great, nonthreatening way to keep the ball rolling. The key is to ask lots of questions. Now, I know there will be times when the prospect just turns up and wants to buy. You may not need to ask a single question to make the sale. But remember, you're not just an order taker. Your purpose should be to achieve something other than just the sale. By asking a few questions, you'll build rapport, and this could stand you in good stead next time that customers needs to buy something else.

Develop the habit of listening attentively to what your prospects have to say. It'll make them feel like you have a genuine interest in them. Give out positive strokes. Don't just stand there looking bored, like so many salespeople do. Be enthusiastic, even if you already have the order. Make sure you understand the question cycle. Question—listen—positive stroke. Make this part of your routine. Get good at it and you'll be amazed at the results you'll achieve.

While asking questions, give out little pieces of information, and talk in the prospect's language.

Depending on the situation or the product or service you're selling, there could be a few more important questions you need to ask. The first has to do with understanding your prospect's authority to arrive at a buying decision. Be sure to ask, "Who other than yourself will be involved in making this decision?" This is particularly relevant if you're selling real estate or cars. Then there's the matter of finances. Ask this question: "Obviously finances are very important. Can I ask what budget you've set aside for this purchase?" The answer to this will not only help you hone in on a suitable price range, it'll also indicate whether the prospect is actually ready to make the buying decision. They may still have to visit the bank to arrange a loan, for instance.

So let's assume now you're at the stage where you can close the sale. You've reached emotion and gathered all the information you need. Ask a question that goes something like this: "Based on what you've told me, (prospect's name), either solution X or solution Y will suit you best."

When you've offered the solution, it's time to check the prospect's temperature with a detailed question. "How does that fit with what you had in mind?" Or, "Which one fits best with what you had in mind?"

At this stage, *assume the sale*. Continue with a question something like this: "Would it be OK if I outlined what we need to get that underway?" Then be silent. Silence here is your greatest asset.

Handling Objections

Selling isn't always smooth sailing. Because most prospects will be looking for points of elimination (especially if they're in the early stages of their purchasing process), they'll be raising objections to your arguments. So, how do you handle these?

With more questions. Get specific, with questions like these:

"Is there any other reason besides. . .?"

"If (reason) was fixed, would it be OK to go ahead?"

If the answer is *no*, there must be another reason. "Can I ask what it is?"

If *yes*, "Let's invest some time looking at (reason)."

Persistence Pays

There will be instances when, despite your best efforts, the prospects just aren't willing or able to make a decision then and there. In cases like this, most salespeople write them off to experience. But don't give up. Persistence here is the key.

Keep in touch with your prospects. Show them that you care. Help them work through the questions that are proving to be sticking points for them. It could be that they still have to reach a decision on whether to buy at all. It may not be your product, service, or price that is the issue. They may have difficulties with finance or authority that need to be resolved first. Keep close to them and assist wherever possible. Build familiarity and rapport. That way, if they eventually do decide to go ahead, you'll be the first person they approach.

Make a point of staying in contact over the phone and though the mail. Mail or fax them a brochure or specification sheets. And be persistent. It usually pays off in the end.

Be Professional

Professionalism is the hallmark of a great salesperson. The more professional you appear, the more prospects will listen to what you have to say. People like dealing with experts in their field, with those who know what they're talking about. They want good advice before buying. They are afraid of being caught by some clever salesperson whose only interest is to make money.

Being professional isn't difficult. All it takes is a genuine desire to help others to buy, and paying some attention to detail in the following areas:

- Developing a good sales kit.
- Dressing well.

- Always being on time.

- Keeping in touch with your prospects.

- Preframing your prospect carefully.

- Doing your homework.

- Keeping testimonials.

- Building rapport.

- Finding out what's most important to your prospect.

- Always following up.

- Asking for referrals.

- Sending thank-you cards.

- Being consistent.

Observe these "rules" and you'll outshine the vast majority of salespeople out there. You'll be one step ahead of them when your prospect comes to making the decision about which company to run with. Get their business, service them well, and you'll be well on your way to developing a band of *raving fans* who will ensure your sales targets are met every month.

You should now have a slightly different perspective of what real *selling* is all about.

Now it's time to concentrate on some of the less obvious areas of the selling process.

"So, does this throw a new light on selling, Charlie?"

"It sure does, Brad. It's blown me away. I had no idea selling was such an involved business. I mean, I thought there was nothing to it—you just started talking to the customers and did the deal if they wanted to buy. But what you've told me has put a whole new light on it. I can fully understand now why those that are good at it—I mean those that understand the process and how people react—can make such a good living."

"And so can you, Charlie. You see, it's not rocket science. Understand the basics and it'll transform your bottom line."

"I think you're right. I feel so stupid, not having even thought to improve on my selling skills before."

"Don't feel bad, Charlie. Like I always say, there's never a better time than right now to start. But selling is just one part of the story. What we're now going to look at are quotes."

Part 2

▪ Quotes

The Nature of Quoting

"I'm sure this is one aspect of the business you're involved in quite heavily, Charlie."

"You're not wrong there, Brad. Customers either expect a quote up front when they book their cars in for work, or, if we discover something that needs attending to during a routine service, we always contact them to get their approval before going ahead. And they always want to know what it's going to cost."

"So they want a quote."

"That's right. And this is one area that determines whether we pick up the extra business or not, so I'm particularly interested in hearing what you have to say."

"Let me get this right. You say gaining additional business hinges on your ability to provide the customer with a good quote?"

"That's exactly right, Brad."

"So you believe that if you shave off just enough margin to make the job attractive, yet not too much so that you make a fair profit, you get the work?"

"Yep."

"You're wrong, Charlie. Listen up. Whether you get the go-ahead or not depends on your selling skills, not the price you quote. I'll guarantee that if you were to actually increase your prices by 10 percent and did a great job in selling, you'll still get the job."

"No way, Brad. No way."

"Trust me. I've actually suggested this strategy to hundreds of businesses and it works. But we're jumping ahead here. Bear with me as we go back to basics."

What Is a Successful Quoting Procedure?

Some businesspeople tend to be unrealistic about the response they receive from their quotes. While some expect a response rate of 90 percent, the reality is that even the best quotes usually only return half that (of course, it also depends on the industry and the number of competing companies).

No matter how good you are as an organization, or how good the deal you're offering is, there are some factors you can't account for. These include things like personal relationships with other suppliers or cash problems.

So, Is a 40 Percent Conversion Rate Unsuccessful?

Not usually. Basically any quoting process that pays for itself can be considered successful. Here's a more in-depth guide to judging the success of your quoting procedure:

1. Work out your costs. This includes the cost of advertising, staff, phone calls, offers, etc.

2. Know your margins. You need to know the net profit you make from anyone who buys your product or service. By understanding how much you actually make from each sale, you'll be able to work out the percentage response required to cover your costs and make you a profit.

3. Lifetime value. Don't view each new customer as a one-time sale. Depending on the industry, you may lose money on the first sale to a new client. The average business will need to sell to a client two times before it begins to make a profit from her. Of course, if you're selling larger items, it can be a different story. Response rate is largely irrelevant—in some cases, a 1 percent response rate is something to be proud of. Here's an example that shows you why. Let's say you run an ad that costs $400—that gets you 100 calls. To sell to those 100 people, it costs you $200 in phone calls and letters. Let's also imagine that the product you're selling is priced at $23,000, with a margin of 40 percent. You'd have to be pretty happy to convert 1 percent of those 100 calls, wouldn't you? That means, for every $9200 you earn, you have to spend $600. That's a pretty good return on investment. At the end of the day, that's all that matters.

What Makes a Successful Quoting Process?

The actual specifics of how to write a great quote process is covered in the next section, but let's get a broad overview now.

The most important thing to consider is this: You are not giving quotes, although that's what people will ask for, and expect. You are providing a Plan of Action—an outline of what will be happening from here on in. The revised title assumes there will be action, and that's a positive assumption to make.

Once you understand this, then it's OK to move on. To start winning more jobs, you need to think outside the box. You must do things differently if you want to achieve better results.

Now, it's critical you take care of the big issues before worrying about little things like what's the best word to use. Here are the four main things to consider when planning a quoting process:

Targeted Lists. You don't want to quote to anyone who would not be interested in your product or service. This may sound obvious, but you'll save a lot of time if you qualify your prospects better.

Process. You need to plan your process. It's unlikely you'll sell large, expensive items in one step, and you're really kidding yourself if you can't close a $50 sale in two steps or less. You may need to add an extra step to get better-qualified leads, or more leads, or an extra phone call to make sure you close a couple more.

Urgency. People can put off buying forever—if you don't give them a reason to act now, your quote will be unlikely to work.

Your Focus. Your process must be focused on the customers. Forget about what you can do. Think about what they want and how you can provide it. Be realistic. Do they want high quality, a great deal, good service, someone who takes an interest in what they want, or something customized and a whole lot of little things. You'll need to find these things out during the process. Don't be pig-headed. Find out what they want, then do it (assuming it's reasonable).

A successful quoting process is based on a successful idea. It doesn't matter which way you try to sell something that is uninteresting, unappealing, and unaffordable—it'll still sound like rubbish. Likewise, if you've got a great offer, a good product, and you've really targeted the market, there's not much you can do to go wrong.

Give some thought to the overall picture first. Is what you're offering really worth the trouble of marketing it? Perhaps you might have to face the hard reality that the reason your business is not succeeding is because it's a bad business. Remember, if your business seems impossible to market, perhaps it is. But by the same token, you never know until you try.

The Five Steps to Winning the Job

Step 1: Who Is Your Target Market?

Before you do anything, you need to identify exactly whom it is you're trying to sell to. Precisely who is your target market?

A failure to answer this question will definitely lead to a poor conversion rate. Imagine a company that sells in-ground swimming pools quoting to someone renting in a block of high-rise apartments. You need to know who your potential customers are before using your script. Knowing your target market will also enable you to speak in a way that your prospects can relate to. Using terms and phrases that are commonly used by your prospects will greatly increase the effectiveness of your Plan of Action.

So let's get specific. Who are the people most likely to be interested in your product or service? Here are some guidelines:

   Age: How old are they? Don't just say "all ages" or "a variety." We want to create a mental picture of your average customer. Think of an age that symbolizes most of them.

   Sex: Are they male or female? "Half and half" is too broad. Practically every business is split one way or the other. Give it some real thought—which gender does business with you currently, and more importantly, what role does gender play? Are they the influencer, information gatherer, or decision maker? Often, you'll have an information gatherer and influencer (usually, a wife) and a decision maker (usually, the husband). Of course, things are often different these days.

Income: How much do they make? Do they earn a great living (meaning quality is the big issue), or are they scraping for every dollar, always looking for a deal? It's essential you find this out.

Where do they live? Are they local, or do they come from miles around to deal with you? This will dictate how you communicate with them.

Education: How do they speak and what do they read? It's important to speak in the way that they do. If you quote to a bunch of bricklayers sounding super officious and highfalutin, they will wonder what planet you're from. You need to tailor your process to suit each situation.

Step 2: How Is Your Process Structured?

Above anything else, you need to develop a system for winning the job. You need to understand you have to have a set procedure to handle quotes. If you're just freestyling every time, you'll quickly fall into a trap. You'll never be able to employ people to take your place, unless they know everything you know and can do everything you can do. If that's the way you want to do it, then good luck!

You also need to test and measure your system until you're 100 percent confident that it works, and that you can predict the results every month. When you can say, "We'll get $54,000 worth of sales this month, so I can afford that new BMW," you've made it. That's the real value of testing and measuring.

Basically, your process can be made up of the following elements:

Lead Generation: This could be either through the Yellow Pages, advertising, personal contact, referral, or something else entirely. Read my book *Instant Leads* to really master this. You need to test and measure this aspect also. You need to be certain you'll get a reasonable number of leads each month from each and every marketing strategy you employ. Of course, while you're doing this you should be simultaneously testing a variety of strategies to find out which works best for you. The other consideration is targeting and qualification—you need to be sure you're getting calls from people who have some chance of buying.

Information: This is the standard "call-for-a-brochure" part, although there are more creative ways to go about it. For example, consider sending out an information booklet on the seven ways to cut your pool's running costs, or five things you must know before choosing a computer programmer for your new software. You could also send out a free tape or video, or a free computer analysis of your business. This step can work well—people like doing things that involve low commitment, and calling for a brochure is the most minimal commitment activity you'll find. It's also good for you as you get people putting their hands up to say, "Yes, I'm kind of interested in that type of thing." You then have their details and can follow them up later.

Initial Consultation: This is where you actually have contact with the customers. You get to discuss their situation and how you can meet their needs. It's also your chance to show how nice you are—people tend to deal with people they like. Sometimes, businesses with higher prices will win the job because they seem "friendly." This is especially true when dealing with female customers. Although men are also interested in being treated well, many women can quickly develop a strong aversion to people who they perceive as sleazy or as rip-off merchants. By the end of the consultation, you need to walk away with a clear picture of what the customer wants and the small issues involved. You may offer the price then and there, and attempt to close immediately. This is covered in more detail later.

Plan of Action: This is the actual quote form you give, or mail, to the customer. There are ways to do it differently. Why not throw in a mention of your guarantee, and the seven reasons to deal with you? You'll find a more detailed explanation later.

Follow-up Phone Call/Letter: It's absolutely essential you have a follow-up process if you are mailing out a Plan of Action. If you don't, you can only blame yourself for a poor conversion rate.

Close/Final Interaction: This is the crux of the matter, although it shouldn't really be. If you've done everything else right up to this point, it should be as simple as saying, "Well, it's clear this is the right thing for you. How will you be paying for it?" You should always ask an open-ended question such as, "Which credit card would you like to put that on?" This isn't being pushy—if you've asked the right questions up until now, and answered all objections, there's no reason why the customers will say "no." You should assume they are ready to buy.

Step 3: What Do You Have to Offer Your Prospects?

Before even attempting to answer the above question, you first need to understand your customers. If you understand their needs, wants, and situations, you can sell almost anything to them.

It's all about taking them from Point A (not knowing if they want to deal with you) right through to Point B (where they hand over their cash).

First, you need to establish where Point A is. What do they already know about you? How do they feel about you? How do they generally feel about your product or service? How often have people in your industry harassed them? Do they want to spend a lot of time or just get it over with? What objections do they have? What else is important?

Put all this together and you'll have an understanding of what the person feels and wants. Of course, everyone's different, but you will have noticed certain patterns—common things most people seem to want. It's important that you put yourself in your customer's shoes. Don't think of them as someone totally different than you. Think about what you do when shopping. You probably know exactly what you want, and you want it for less than you thought you'd have to pay for it. This is natural. People want the most they can get for the least they have to give. That's fine—it's human nature.

So, does this mean you have to give away your goods and services for below cost just to make a sale? No, but you have to be *seen* to be providing a good deal. People want to feel they've "won." This is especially true with men. They seem to want to feel they've beaten the dealer and scored an amazing deal. For proof of this, just watch men shopping for a car—unless they feel they've screwed the dealer into the ground, they're not interested.

As a business owner, that can be pretty disheartening—but be realistic, isn't that what you do to other businesses? More than the desire to get a great deal, people don't want to feel they're being ripped off. That's part of the reason they want to get a better deal—they're always so certain you're making a killing from the sale, so why should you get all that money? Beyond all this, people want something else. They want the benefit of whatever they're buying. For example, when buying a car, people want transportation, reliability, power, prestige, and control. These aren't features of the car—they're the actual benefits of owning the car. People aren't buying a car; they're buying transportation. And in the case of a BMW or Ferrari, they're buying a fast, hot-looking mode of transportation.

Thinking about that, it's clear people will pay more if you give them more benefit. If your car looks better, and will be more reliable, you can probably charge more. This is the whole price-issue argument in a nutshell. If you find out what the customer's main motivation is, then fulfill that to the maximum, you'll find that person will pay more. If you satisfy her in this way and then sweeten the deal, you'll win the job almost every time.

So how do you find out what the customers' main motivation is? Simple— you need to talk to them and ask them a lot of questions. It's always amazing to see businesses that give quotes without really asking any questions. I'm not surprised they don't win many jobs. The best question to ask is this: "OK, what's most important to you in this buying decision?" Or ask this: "What are you looking for most in your new [x]?" How about this: "What are you going to use this [y] for?"

Once they've answered these questions, repeat the answer back to them.

"Right, so beyond everything else, you're looking for an [x] that will do [y]." If they answer positively, you've just been given the game plan. Gear your process towards fulfilling this desire. Refer back to it at all stages, and dispel all competitors by suggesting that their alternative will not do the job as well as yours will. Of course, this has to be *true*. If you honestly can't satisfy the customer as well as a competitor can, you may be wasting your time even quoting to them.

If it turns out you can help the customer, you need to work out how you're going to encourage them to buy from you—and soon. It pays to remember that simply asking people to act now (or for that matter, telling them to act now) is rarely enough. You need to give them a good reason why *now* is the time to do something. If people have come to you through the Yellow Pages or another lead generation method, this won't be such a challenge, as they've put their hand up to say, "I'm ready to buy."

Even so, most purchases (especially those of a luxury nature) can be delayed forever. It's one thing to fulfill the desires, but it's another to actually get people to part with their cash. In many cases, your biggest competitor is *nonaction*— when people decide not to go ahead.

Every month, customers have to decide what to spend their money on. It could very realistically be a decision between buying a patio from you, and clearing their dangerously high credit card debt. Every buyer has priorities. Of course, there are ways of rearranging these priorities. If you offer a special deal on the patio, the customer may think, "Well, the bank will let me off for a bit longer, but I won't get this deal on the patio again."

The question is, how do you offer a great deal without slicing your profit margin drastically? There are a couple of ways. First, make sure you are selling products or services with a high margin. If you have the option of gearing your business towards higher-margin items, do so, as it makes it much easier to come up with great deals. If you can't, you need to find items or services that are highly valued by your customers, yet have a low cost. Extra service is an old standby. Information booklets are another. A great price is common, although it can be a double-edged sword, as people will often ask your competitors to match it (and as you know, they probably will).

There are two ways to escape the price game. First, offer a deal that your competitors can't. For example, if you sell computer systems, offer a software program that you've designed—free. Secondly (and more reliably), give your customers more of what they want. Simply be everything they want, then offer them a reasonable deal. The aim is for them to say, "Well, these guys are a little bit more expensive, but they do [x], [y] and [z]."

Of course, you can create urgency by placing a limitation on availability. You could say, "These will be available only for the next two weeks, then the new model is coming out." "The prices are about to rise," is another great way of forcing people to act. Or say, "We'll only be in town for the next four days." Naturally, being truthful is better, as people are excellent at picking up insincerity.

Step 4: How Do You Win the Job?

From the last few sections, something should be abundantly clear; if you want to win the job, you must give people what they want and make them feel like they're getting a great deal. If you just offer a price, people will always find someone to beat it. If you offer them no reasons to buy from you, they won't. Let's be real— it can be tough.

There are people out there willing to sell stuff under cost just to get cashflow. These same people close up shop three months later, but in the short term, they can create havoc for you.

So what can you do to ensure that you win the job, even when people are undercutting you in such a drastic way?

First, let's examine your process. Are you giving people too little information, or too much? If your leads aren't sure whether they want to deal with you, you haven't given them enough. If you call them and they say, "I've already bought from someone else," you've probably missed the boat by giving them too much information.

Here's a guide to three different processes you could take. I call them the long, the medium, and the short. You may see some steps you're missing, or perhaps the shorter process will show you that your sale could be made quicker and easier. Of course, there's much in common between them, so just choose the process that suits you best.

Let's start by examining the short process.

Short Process

Lead Generation: This will generally be the result of strategies such as the Yellow Pages, advertising, personal contact, referrals, or something else entirely. You need to test and measure this aspect, as you need to be certain you'll get a reasonable number of leads per month from each marketing strategy you put in place. Of course, you should be simultaneously testing a variety of strategies. The other consideration is targeting and qualification. You need to be sure you're getting calls from people who have some chance of buying.

Taking a Phone Inquiry: Include a greeting that announces your name, your company, and thanks the prospect for calling. Say, "Hi, thanks for calling [business name], this is [your full name]." Slow down with this part. If you seem to be rushing through, it'll set the tone for the entire call.

Get into the Questions: Whatever they ask first, make sure you say, "Thanks for your call. Just so I can help you best, is it OK if I ask you a couple of questions?" Don't answer their initial question under any circumstances.

Ask Open-Ended Questions: Without doubt, this is the most important thing anyone could ever learn about scripts. You must ask questions that can't be answered with a straight "yes" or "no," or questions the prospects have to think about and get involved in. It's a good idea to ask questions that encourage the prospects to do the selling for you. Ask them specifically what they need, who else they've seen, how much they think is a fair price to pay, that sort of thing. Then tell them about how good you are. Ask them this: "And what benefits can you see in having a business that will do all that for you?" It's a tricky way to get them to say, "Yes, it would be a good idea to deal with you."

Get Agreement: At some point, you must get some feedback from the prospect. The best way to do this is to ask a rhetorical question, and get them to answer, "Yes." This is the one time you break the rules. You say, "So it sounds like you'd benefit by [benefit 1], [benefit 2], and [benefit 3]—that sounds pretty irresistible, doesn't it?" Or, using a softer approach, what about, "You can see the sense in what I'm saying, can't you?"

Deal with Objections: To get into this part, ask the question, "So you're OK to go ahead with the proposal I've suggested?" You might get lucky. More likely, the prospect will probably raise an objection or two. That's fine—as long as you know how to deal with them. The first thing that you say is this: "Can you elaborate on that for me?" Get them talking a bit more. Then say something like this: "Now, assuming I could show you a way to get around that problem, would you be interested in that information?" Then answer the objection, but do it empathetically—that is, say, "I understand that, and I used to think that way myself, but then I discovered (x)," or alternately, "Yes, I know what you mean. Someone else said that to me recently, but here's something that will surprise you."

Then it's really up to you. You need to determine the major objections and a way to acknowledge them before turning them around. If someone says, "I haven't got the money," you could say, "I understand that—it's usually short this time of year. But there's some good news—you can afford this. We have layaway, payment plans, and interest-free finance for six months. We also accept all major credit cards. Which of those would be most suitable for you?"

If he replies, "I don't have time," you could say, "Yes, it's hard to find time when life is so busy—but you know what, it only takes one hour a week, and the benefits are incredible. Wouldn't you say it's worth investing just one hour in yourself? You know, doing something just for *you?*"

Of course, there'll be times when you run into objections that can't be answered. If you offer your best payment plans and your customers still can't afford it, then forget it. If they've just bought a competitor's brand and would never change, forget it too. These people aren't in your target market, and should be scratched from your list.

Remember, you can't sell to people who don't have the means to buy, or no interest in doing so.

Close and Take the Next Step: If you've gotten this far, you should be able to assume that the people are interested in buying. If you have agreement and you've dealt with their objections, it's time to nail it down. The first thing to do is try an assumptive close. That is, "We'll make an appointment now—would you prefer tomorrow or Thursday?" You could say, "OK, which credit card is it easiest to process that on?"

Something else to consider is making the decision for them. Instead of saying, "Would you like to book your service now?" why not say, "I'd like to book you in for your service now—would today or tomorrow suit you better?"

If your close fails and they say, "No, not yet," or "I don't want to," say, "OK, I thought you were ready to get the process under way. Level with me—what's preventing you making this decision right now?" Or alternately, "What is it you're not telling me?"

Medium Process

Lead Generation: Once again, this is through the Yellow Pages, advertising, personal contact, referral, or something else entirely. You need to test and measure this aspect, as you need to be certain you'll get a reasonable number of leads per month from each marketing strategy. Of course, you should be simultaneously testing a variety of strategies. The other consideration is targeting and qualification. You need to be sure you're getting calls from people who have some chance of buying.

Taking a Phone Inquiry: Include a greeting that announces your name, your company, and thanks the prospect for calling. Say, "Hi, thanks for calling [business name]. This is [your full name]." Slow down with this part. If you seem to be rushing through it, it'll set the tone for the rest of the call.

Get into the Questions: Whatever they ask first, make sure you say, "Thanks for your call. Just so I can help you best, is it OK if I ask you a couple of questions?" Don't under any circumstances answer their initial question.

Ask Open-Ended Questions: You must ask questions that can't be answered with a straight "yes" or "no." Questions the prospect has to think about and get involved in. It's a good idea to ask questions that encourage the prospects to do the selling for you. Ask them specifically what they need, who else they've seen, and how much they think is a fair price to pay, etc. Then tell them about how good you are. Ask, "And what benefits can you see in having a business that will do all that for you?" It's a tricky way to get them to say, "Yes, it would be a good idea to deal with you."

Make an Appointment Time: Simply say, "OK, it sounds like we can help you—I can come out and see you on Thursday night or Friday morning. Which of those suits you best?"

Initial Consultation: This is where you actually have contact with the customers, discuss their situation, and how you can meet their needs. It's also your chance to show how nice you are—people tend to deal with people they like. Sometimes, businesses with higher prices will win the job because they seem "friendly." This is especially true when dealing with female customers. By the end of the consultation, you need to walk away with a clear picture of what the customer wants as well as the small issues.

Plan of Action: This is the actual quote form you give or mail to the customer. There are ways to do this differently. Why not throw in a mention of your guarantee, and the seven reasons to deal with you? You'll find a more detailed explanation later.

Make a Second Appointment: Simply call and say, "I'm out that way tomorrow. I'll stop by and run over the proposal with you. Would you prefer 2:00 p.m. or 4:00 p.m.?"

Deal with Objections: To get into this part, ask the question, "So you're OK to go ahead with the proposal we discussed?" You never know; they might say yes, but more likely, the prospects will probably raise an objection. That's fine—as long as you know how to deal with it. The first thing you say is this: "Can you elaborate on that for me?" Get them talking a bit more. Then say something like this: "Now, assuming I could show you a way to get around that problem, would you be interested in that information?"

Then answer the objection, but do it empathetically—that is, say, "I understand that, and I used to think that way myself, but then I discovered (x)." Or alternately, "Yes, I know what you mean. Someone else said that to me recently, but here's something that will surprise you." Then, it's really up to you. You need to determine the major objections and a way to acknowledge them before turning them around. If someone says, "I haven't got the money," you could say, "I understand that—it's usually short this time of year. But there's some good news—you can afford this. We have layaway, payment plans, and interest-free finance for six months. We also accept all major credit cards. Which of those would be most suitable for you?"

If customers say, "I don't have time," you could respond, "Yes, it's hard to find time when life is so busy—but you know what, it only takes one hour a week, and the benefits are incredible. Wouldn't you say it's worth investing just one hour in yourself? You know, doing something just for *you?*"

Of course, there'll be times when you run into objections that can't be answered. If you offer your best payment plans and they still can't afford it, then forget it. If they've just bought a competitor's brand and would never change, forget it too. These people aren't in your target market, and should be scratched from your list.

Remember, you can't sell to people who don't have the means to buy, or the interest in doing so.

Close/Final Interaction: This is the crux of the matter, although it shouldn't really be. If you've done everything else right up to this point, it should be as simple as, "OK, so have you got your checkbook with you? Great—let's do the deal."

If you haven't developed the relationship to the point where you can say that, you need to ask yourself why. You've spoken to the customers five or six times already, so they should be quite friendly by now. The other thing to consider is that people will feel a weight lifting from their shoulders when they decide to go with you—their decision is over.

Long Process

Lead Generation: Either Yellow Pages, advertising, personal contact, referral, or something else entirely. You need to test and measure this aspect, as you need to be certain you'll get a reasonable number of leads per month from each marketing strategy. Of course, you should be simultaneously testing a variety of strategies. The other consideration is targeting and qualification. You need to be sure you're getting calls from people who have some chance of buying.

Take Phone Inquiries: Include a greeting that announces your name, your company, and thanks the prospect for calling. Say, "Hi, thanks for calling [business name]. This is [your full name]." Slow down with this part. If you seem to be rushing through it, it'll set the tone for the entire call.

Get into the Questions: Whatever they ask first, make sure you say, "Thanks for your call. Just so I can help you best, is it OK if I ask you a couple of questions?" Don't, under any circumstances, answer their initial question.

Ask Open-Ended Questions: You must ask questions that can't be answered with a straight "yes" or "no"—questions the prospect has to think about and get involved in. It's a good idea to ask questions that encourage the prospects to do the selling for you. Ask them specifically what they need, who else they've seen, how much they think is a fair price to pay, etc. Then tell them about how good you are. Ask them this: "And what benefits can you see in having a business that will do all that for you?" It's a tricky way to get them to say, "Yes, it would be a good idea to deal with you."

Send Information: This is the standard "send-them-a-brochure" part, although there are more creative ways to go about it. An information booklet (seven ways to cut your pool running costs, five things you must know before choosing a computer programmer for your new software), a free tape or video, or a free computer analysis of your business, works very well in this regard. People like doing things that involve low commitment, and calling for a brochure is the most minimal commitment activity you'll find. It's also good for you as you get people putting their hands up to say, "Yes, I'm kind of interested in that type of thing." You then have their details and can follow them up later.

Follow-up Information: Call up and ask for the chance to see them. First, ask about the information—what did they like about it? If they haven't gone through it yet, outline the main parts, and then ask them what benefits they see in what you've just said. Keep asking questions that have a "yes" answer, such as, "It would be a good idea to see how much that is, don't you agree?" Once you have basic agreement, lead into the next part. "Look, I'm out that way next week. I could come out Thursday night or Friday morning—which of those suits you better?" Set a time and write it in your appointment book.

Initial Consultation: This is where you actually have contact with the customers, discussing their situation, and how you can meet their needs. It's also your chance to show how nice you are. People tend to deal with people that they like. Sometimes, businesses with higher prices will win the job because they seem "friendly." By the end of the consultation, you need to walk away with a clear picture of what the customer wants as well as the small issues involved.

Plan of Action: This is the actual quote form you give or mail to the customer. There are ways to do this differently. Why not throw in a mention of your guarantee, and the seven reasons to deal with you?

Phone the Customer: It's absolutely essential you have a follow-up process in place, if you are mailing out a Plan of Action. If you don't, you can only blame yourself for a poor conversion rate.

Outline Reason for Call: You must explain why you are calling, but always ask for permission first. Say, "Is it OK if I outline the reason for my call today?" Then do exactly that. Explain the process you'll be running through, then ask if it's OK if you go through the call that way. People tend to be a bit confused by this approach, but that's a good thing. You want to stand out by saying, "This is something different, and I'm a professional."

Get Agreement: At some point, you must get some feedback from your prospect. The best way is to ask a rhetorical question, and getting them to answer "yes." This is the one time you break the rules. You say, "So it sounds like you'd benefit by [benefit 1], [benefit 2], and [benefit 3]— that sounds pretty irresistible, doesn't it?" Or, as a softer approach, what about this: "You can see the sense in what I'm saying, can't you?"

Deal with Objections: To get into this part, ask the question, "So you're OK to go ahead with the proposal we discussed?" Most probably, the prospects will raise an objection at this point. That's fine, as long as you know how to deal with it.

The first thing you say is this: "Can you elaborate on that for me?" Get them talking a bit more. Then say something like, "Now, assuming I could show you a way to get around that problem, would you be interested in that information?" Then answer the objection, but do it empathetically—that is, say, "I understand that, and I used to think that way myself, but then I discovered. . ." Or alternately, "Yes, I know what you mean. Someone else said that to me recently, but here's something that will surprise you." Then it's really up to you. You need to determine the major objections and a way of acknowledging them before turning them around.

If someone says, "I haven't got the money," you could respond by saying, "I understand that—it's usually short this time of year. But there's some good news. You can afford this. We have layaway, payment plans, and interest-free finance for six months. We also accept all major credit cards. Which of those would be most suitable for you?" If they say, "I don't have time," you could say, "Yes, it's hard to find time when life is so busy—but you know what, it only takes one hour a week, and the benefits are incredible. Wouldn't you say it's worth investing just one hour in yourself? You know—doing something just for *you?*"

Of course, there'll be times when you run into objections that can't be answered. If you offer your best payment plans and they still can't afford it, then forget it. If they've just bought a competitor's brand and would never change, forget it too. These people aren't in your target market, and should be scratched from your list. Remember, you can't sell to people who don't have the means to buy, or who have no interest in doing so.

Close and Take the Next Step: If you've gotten this far, you should be able to assume that the people are interested in buying. If you have agreement and you've dealt with their objections, it's time to nail the sale down. The first thing to do is try an assumptive close. That is, "We'll make an appointment now—would you prefer tomorrow or Thursday?" Or, "OK, which credit card is it easiest to process that on?" Something else to consider is making the decision for them. Instead of saying, "Would you like to book your service now?" why not say, "I'd like to book you in for your service now—would today or tomorrow suit you better?" If your close fails and they say, "No, not yet," or "I don't want to," say, "OK, I thought you were ready to get the process under way. Level with me—what's preventing you from making this decision right now? What is it that you're not telling me?"

Close/Final Interaction: This is the crux of the entire process, although it really shouldn't be. If you've done everything else correctly up to this point, it should as simple as saying, "OK, so have you got your check book with you? Great—let's do the deal."

If you haven't developed the relationship to the point where you can say this, you need to ask yourself why. You've spoken to the customer five or six times already, so they should be quite friendly by now. The other thing to consider is that people will feel a weight lifting from their shoulders when they decide to go with you—their decision is over.

Once you've gotten your process organized, you need to create systems for each part. That is—how do you answer the phone *every* time, what does your quote form look like, what words do you use to close the sale?

Here are some guidelines for the common parts of the process:

First Interaction: Create a system that ensures people will know you are friendly and professional. For example, have a standard joke you always use, like: "So you're interested in a new car? I guess the hubby wants something red, huh?" A word of advice, though—don't use this line under any circumstances. Come up with something that's actually amusing. Also, make sure you listen to the people. Ask them lots of questions, and really take an interest. Pretend you're a friend trying to help them. This may sound strange, but give it a go. You may be surprised.

Quote Form/Plan of Action: There's no rule that says every quote form must look exactly the same. In fact, there are no rules at all. Your quote can look like anything at all, and you can include anything you like. It's mystifying why businesses don't do most of their advertising on their quote forms. This is the place where people actually make the decision. There's no reason not to put something like, "Even if you've found someone who'll do it cheaper, here are seven reasons to go with us." Or what about, "If you're not sure whether you should buy from us, here are three facts that will help you decide."

Remember, if someone else is doing a better deal with a better product and a stronger guarantee, you're not going to win the job. You can simply forget it. Don't even worry about what your quote form looks like. Go back to the drawing board on your business. And here's something that's essential for small businesses: people will *not* deal with you just because you're local and small. These days, people prefer big companies. They have a security that a small business can't offer. If you want people to deal with you, you'll have to do better than saying you're local and will give better service. You have to *stand out*!

There are a couple of tricks you can use to win the job. These are "out-of-the-box" ideas that break the mold and can truly get you out of the price game. One idea is the "two-deal" approach. That is, offer the customer the choice of two deals. The first is high priced and full featured. It's still good value, but it's definitely not for a pensioner. The second offer is cheaper and more basic. In many ways, this can double your chances of winning the job, as it's almost like setting yourself up as two businesses. Make sure each deal fits with the customer's needs.

Another approach is the "no-price" method. This is particularly cheeky. You offer to mail the customer a quote. Your quote form contains no price—only an outline of your proposal and the reasons why people should deal with you. You explain the absence of the price with this: "I want you to have it all—the best price and the best quality. That's why I'm not going to give you a price yet. I'll phone in two days to find out what other prices you've received, then offer you something just as good."

People sometimes worry about whether they have the ability to write anything beyond the normal quote form. It might sound funny, but most people won't even know if you're using proper English or not. People are not likely to avoid buying from you because you can't spell "quixotic," "superfluous," or "rhetorical." As long as your message is clear, quick, and well targeted, your Plan of Action will work. It's really like serving food; if you are serving a delicious meal, it'll taste just as good delivered on paper plates as on your best china. People may prefer it on the china, but if you're serving to people hungry for what you've cooked, they'll eat anyway.

There is only one sin you don't want to commit, and that's the sin of getting off the point or rambling for too long. If every word and every sentence says something important about the sale, fine. If your letter is full of guff, people will lose interest very quickly.

We'll get to some examples of powerful Plans of Action soon. When you read through them, you'll notice that the language is kept simple and the ideas quite basic. You should be able to adapt these to your own business.

Of course, there's no need to send out a Plan of Action at all. Taking a different tack entirely, you could offer to come out and see the customers again, explaining you have an idea of the price, but just need to finalize a couple of things. When you get there, you can build a stronger relationship. Just casually ask, "So what's your best deal so far?" Sit down and get to the bottom of what they want, and then do the deal on the spot.

Closing the Sale: This is where so many people fall down. The main reason is that they don't ask for the sale, or they don't ask for it in the right way. They keep getting the "I'll think about it," or "I'll call you back," reply.

The question is, what do they need to think about? If you've answered every objection, why aren't they ready to buy? You need to ask more questions. "OK, I thought you were pretty positive about the proposal. What is it that's preventing you from making this decision?" Or, "You seem unsure about it—what don't you like about our proposal?"

Whatever they say, show them a way around it, and then say, "How does that fit with what you have in mind?" Alternately, you can cut right to the chase and say, "What do I have to offer you to win your business today?" Or why not say, "Look, I really want to do this deal with you. Give me some guidance; what else do you want?"

Once you've dealt with the objections, you can then proceed to the final question. And always use an assumptive close. Here are some good examples:

"So, which credit card is it easiest to process that on?"

"Would you like to pay that off over six months, or will you pay in full today?"

"OK, I'll get that out to you today. What's the best address to deliver it to?"

Always assume that they've decided, and you're now just clarifying the details. If you've been through the whole process successfully, this should be easy to do.

Step 5: What Else Do You Need to Think About?

Use this section as a final checklist. Once you're happy with your new process, run through and make sure you're ready to get started. Here are a few things you may not have thought of:

Team Training: Do your team members fully understand the new process? It's important that they understand the vital role they are to play in this strategy. If your new customers come in and find them uninterested in providing service, the exercise will be a waste of time. Your team members also need to be shown how to use the scripts and Plan of Action. They'll need *lots* of practice. It'll represent a new way of going about their daily tasks, so give them time to adjust.

Check Stock and Team Levels: It's unlikely your new process will make hundreds and hundreds of extra sales all at once (very few actually do), but you need to be prepared for a sizeable response. There would be nothing worse than having a rush of new sales, only to find you have no stock or are too busy to fill the orders.

"Brad, I'm astonished. And you're right; there is more to it than just rattling off a few prices and hoping."

"I'm glad you see the potential, Charlie. So what are you going to do about it?"

"I'm going to draft a quote here and now, Brad. Give me a few minutes, then tell me what you think."

This is Charlie's draft:

A Warning from Charlie's Garage

Good morning, Mr. Jones.

Thanks for booking your car in for a service yesterday. And as this was your first visit to Charlie's Garage, the only thing you paid for were the parts used.

I'd like to remind you of our postservice discussion.

The repairs we discussed are important. Our report indicates that you have two serious problems, plus a range of smaller faults.

These problems are *not* life-threatening, but they are endangering you, and are in need of quick attention.

Here's why:

Your suspension takes a battering every day—each time you drive your car over a pothole, up a gutter, or even on an extra bumpy road, it needs to be performing at 100 percent, or you're in danger.

Faulty suspension parts can wear out quickly, and cause much larger problems—in the extreme case, a complete failure, which means you'll lose control of the car. In the mild case, your tires will wear out four times as fast, which means you'll be hit in the wallet.

Similarly, a leaking exhaust can cause drowsiness, particularly if the toxic emissions seep into the car through ill-fitting door or trunk seals.

Because of the reasons I've outlined above, it worries me that you haven't yet booked your car in for the work we discussed.

I understand it's a blow to your budget, but the work *will* need to be done at some point. I'd recommend you do it sooner, rather than many hours of driving later.

Every time you drive your car, you are placing the worn parts under more stress, and greatly increasing the chance they will fail altogether.

But let me make this clear—it is *not* my intention to scare you, but rather to alert you to the facts.

Following our check, we determined the following work should be carried out as a matter of urgency:

Fit new front shock absorbers
Fit a new muffler
Replace worn distributor cap
Flush the radiator

As a special incentive to come back to Charlie's Garage in the next 14 days (and provide yourself with the peace of mind every car owner should have), I'm more than happy to replace the distributor cap and flush the radiator FREE when you have the rest of the work done. The price for the complete job will be $370.00, which includes parts and labor.

I'll give you a call in the next few days and we'll discuss this further.

Charlie

Proprietor, Charlie's Garage

P.S. We have credit card facilities, and the option of a three-month payment plan.

Examples

RE: Your new home, 22 Watford Street.

Dear [name],

I thought I'd mail you a couple of tea bags and a muffin with this letter. Here's why: Who you build with is a serious decision, and one worth considering for the few brief moments it takes to enjoy a tea break.

So put the kettle on, and think seriously about what you want from your builder.

Before going into that, I'll get the financial details out of the way. To build the home we discussed, the investment is $229,748 (you'll find the precise details on the bottom of page 2).

While "what's the price?" is an important question, here are a few others worth asking:

1) Does your builder offer a guarantee on completion time, *and* offer to pay your rent for every week the project runs overtime?

2) Does your builder promise that every aspect of the work will represent quality workmanship, and offer to fix any problems within 24 hours at no charge?

3) Is your builder flexible enough to meet your every need, and willing to alter the design as many times as it takes for you to be absolutely thrilled with the design?

4) Can your builder offer over 100 references from delighted past clients?

5) Is your builder registered with the Master Builders Association, and does your builder use only accredited tradesmen to ensure unquestioned quality?

Of course, I wouldn't be leading you down this path, if Contract Construction didn't fulfill all of the criteria above.

We aim to be one step above the normal builder. Our designs are built with *you* in mind. The same applies to the way we work—we do everything in our power to ensure that your home is ready on time, and we do everything to ensure that you're completely happy with it.

You'll also be constantly updated on the progress of your home and are welcome to visit the construction site at any time. The foreman will explain exactly what's going on, and why.

It means the home you envision is the home you move into.

I'll phone you directly within the next three days to answer any questions you have. We'll discuss where you're up to in the decision-making process, and take it from there.

I look forward to speaking with you soon,

Peter van Eekelen

Contract Constructions

P.S. The price quote is for the design that you have identified as being most ideal. If this is within your budget, I am pleased to say that we have the staff and resources to start work immediately. If not, I'd like the opportunity to design something more affordable for you.

The four most important reasons you should choose Abetta Carpet (the price is only #3).

Hi there,

Before I run through the four reasons in more depth, let me explain what this is all about.

I've noticed that other carpet suppliers tend to just do a "quote"—that is, they give you a price and that's all, as if price is the only thing worth considering when buying carpet.

If all carpeting were the same, that'd be true.

In reality, there are significant differences—things that matter—like how the carpet feels under your feet, whether it stains, how well it's been stitched, if it's resistant to pests and, critically, how many years it will last.

Not to mention the important differences between carpet stores—like whether they use qualified and experienced tradespeople to lay your carpet, whether they guarantee to lay on the date and at the time they promised, whether they offer an iron-clad warranty, and so on.

In the end, it's worth the extra five minutes it takes to consider more than the price.

After all, this is carpeting you'll probably be living with for the next five years and beyond.

With that in mind, sit down with a cup of tea (I've included a couple of teabags for you and [wife's name]) and examine the four most important reasons to deal with Abetta.

1. Abetta offers an unbeatable three-point guarantee. First, all carpet comes with a five-year warranty. Second, our workmanship is guaranteed for a lifetime. Third, we promise you the very best service and advice.

2. Your carpet is laid in less than 8 hours, meaning everything's completed in one day. On top of that, it's ready to walk on immediately.

3. Your investment is just _____, complete. This includes everything we discussed, _____ meters/yards of _____ _____ carpet, delivered, laid, and guaranteed.

4. We deliver your carpet *free* and employ experienced, qualified, and dedicated layers to do the job—no 'backyard boys' to do a half-hearted job. Abetta ensures that your carpet is laid perfectly, and that everything fits immaculately.

Obviously, you'll need some time to think it over— I don't want you to rush. This is a major purchase, and it requires the right amount of thought.

Thanks for the opportunity, and I look forward to a long and happy association.

Eliseo Censori

Abetta Carpets

P.S. You'll notice I've included a small gift pack. Hope you appreciate it. Along with the teabags, you should find a small bottle of spot cleaner, a box of chocolates, and a gift voucher towards your next carpet cleaning. These goodies are yours to keep.

NAME
ADDRESS

Here's why Cloud 9 Tanks should be YOUR first choice. . .

Good afternoon NAME,

I enjoyed speaking with you on [day]. It's always great to come out and show people the Cloud 9 difference. Let me just remind you what that is.

1. You get a 25-year guarantee through Cloud 9—this means your water tank will remain in perfect condition for at least this long. It won't rust, warp, crack, or fail you in any way. Should that happen, we'll come out and replace it within 48 hours.

2. Your tank is made from tough, maintenance-free polyethylene. This is an attractive material that requires no maintenance. More than that, you don't get that "rusty" taste with your water—it tastes pure, clean and fresh—just as nature intended.

3. You can get a full range of accessories through Cloud 9—sprinkler systems, animal troughs, children's pools, underground tanks, pressure pumps, and more, all perfectly integrated and designed to work together.

Your investment in the system we discussed will be [price]. This includes your [size and color] tank, as well as [other inclusions and details]. I guess when you consider that you are buying a lifetime of maintenance-free rainwater storage, it makes good sense. And let me tell you something else. . .

New council regulations mean every resident will now have to pay for the water they use—unless you supply your own, of course. This means that your tank will ultimately pay for itself. And I bet you've already considered the health benefits of drinking and showering in pure rainwater. You just feel "fresher" somehow.

So here's what I plan to do:

I'll call you in a couple of days to confirm our next step. We'll discuss when you're looking to install the tank and any other needs you might have. I'm sure you'll find that Cloud 9 can help.

Until then, all the best.

Ashleigh Mann

Owner, Cloud 9 Tanks

P.S. I spoke to a lady last week who's just installed a Cloud 9 Tank. She's just worked out that, with the saving in her water bills, her tank will actually pay for itself *this year*—true story.

P.P.S. If you've already made up your mind, you might want to call me now. You can reach me at XXX XXXX, or [mobile number] anytime.

Bradley J. Sugars

NAME
ADDRESS

Osborne Park 3:23 p.m.

Together, we'll build your dream home.

Good afternoon, [NAME],

It was great to speak with you last [day]. It's clear that our ideas on design and style are strongly aligned.

Which leads me to the main point.

From our meeting, I'm now confident that you'll be happy in an HBM home. The design we discussed seems to suit your needs perfectly. And for an overall investment of [price], I'm positive that an HBM home is right for you.

Before you make your decision though, here are four things you can expect from HBM:

1. Your home will be completed on the day we promise. If for some reason that's impossible, we'll pay your rent for every day the project runs overtime.

2. Your home will be completed for [price]—there are no surprises or hidden costs.

3. You *will* be delighted. If you don't walk into your completed HBM home and say, "*Wow!*," we'll do whatever it takes to make you happy.

4. Your home comes with a comprehensive 20-year structural guarantee.

This is a serious decision, and HBM understands that, which is why we take the time to give you all the information—not just a price. We want you to move into your HBM home and be ecstatic with the results. So here's what you need to do:

Look through the following list of features and the design I've had specially done up for you. If there's anything you'd like added, removed, or modified, call me immediately. I'll call in a professional architect to make the changes for you.

And here's why I'm doing this for you.

I want your new home to be *exactly* what you want. After all, you're in the process of building a place where you'll spend 50 percent of your time, where you'll store your most treasured possessions, where you'll house your family. It pays to give it some serious thought.

Here are the features of the design we discussed.

1. ....

2. ....

3. ....

4. ....

Remember, [NAME], if there's anything you'd like changed, call me now. I'll have our architect, [architect's name], make the alterations.

On the other hand, you may be thrilled with the design we have. If that's the case, call me and we'll take the next step. But remember, I don't want to start work on your new home until you're completely satisfied. Until you're sure that your HBM home is the best you could possibly have, I don't want you to commit to anything.

Call me at (XXX) XXX XXXX and we'll take the next step now.

Once again, I've enjoyed working with you on this project, and look forward to turning your dream into a reality. Until we speak, all the best.

Gavin Brackenreg
Owner, HBM Homes

P.S. Call me this week and we'll arrange a "virtual reality" tour of your new home. This is where we create a 3-D computer model of your home. You can go through it, room by room, looking at the inside and outside from any angle. This service normally costs $79.00. When you call me this week, it's yours *free*.

P.P.S. Call within the next three days to confirm and you'll receive a special housewarming gift. I'm certain you'll love it—but you must call within the next three days to qualify for this special offer.

P.P.P.S. If I don't hear from you during next week, I'll give you a call, just to see how things are going.

Break-Even Analysis

It's essential that you work out your costs up front. Otherwise, you'll have no idea what you need to achieve in order for the process to be worthwhile. You may find out after doing the analysis that the process costs you so much that it's not worth the trouble.

This analysis is for the whole campaign. After you've worked out your total fixed costs (for the campaign), you then work out your profit (your average dollar sale minus your variable costs), which gives you enough information to work out how many responses you need in order to break even.

Divide this number by the total number of prospects you are planning to approach. This will give you a percentage response rate. As a very rough guide (every case is different), anything over 40 percent is stretching it. If you need that high a response, you might need to rethink your campaign.

The very best businesses get around 40 percent. These are rare results. If you need higher than that to break even, reassess whether this is the best marketing method for you.

Quoting Process
Hard Costs

Advertising	$ . . . .
Envelopes	$ . . . .
Paper	$ . . . .
Printing	$ . . . .
Postage	$ . . . .
Other	$ . . . .
1. Total Fixed Costs	$ . . . .
2. Average $$$ Sale	$ . . . .

Variable Costs

Telephone	$ . . . .
Wages	$ . . . .
Electricity	$ . . . .
Rent	$ . . . .

Brochures $ . . . .

Other Postage $ . . . .

Other $ . . . .

3. Total Variables $ . . . .

Delivery Costs

Cost of Goods Sold $ . . . .

Taxes $ . . . .

Transportation $ . . . .

Packaging $ . . . .

Other $ . . . .

4. Total Delivery $ . . . .

5. Net Profit [2/(3+4)] $ . . . .

6. Conversion Needed to Break Even (1/5) $ . . . .

$$\boxed{\textbf{Part 3}}$$

∎ Scripts

The Nature of Scripts

"Charlie, I'm now going to discuss another important, yet little understood, selling tool, and that's the script."

"The what?"

"The script. A script is nothing more than a carefully thought-out and written down set of questions to use every time someone phones in. They're particularly useful as they ensure you don't get sidetracked and forget to ask the caller whatever it is you need to know."

"But isn't it they who need to know something, Brad?"

"Yes and no. You should use every contact you make to gather, at the very least, information for your database. But you might be interested in finding out other things like which ad is working, what prospects think of specials you may be running, or how they heard about you. Get it?"

"Ah, now I understand, Brad. Communication is always a two-way street."

You're catching on fast, Charlie. So lets get into it then, shall we?"

What Is a Successful Script?

Some businesspeople tend to be overoptimistic about the response they hope they'll get from their scripts. While some expect a response rate of 75–80 percent, the reality is that most scripts will only return a fraction of that.

Does this make them unsuccessful?

No. Basically any script that pays for itself can be considered successful. Here's a more in-depth guide to judging the success of your script:

1. Work out your costs. This includes the cost of advertising, staff, phone calls, offers, etc.

2. Know your margins. You need to know the net profit you make from anyone who buys your product or service. By understanding how much you actually make from each sale, you'll be able to work out the percentage response required from the script.

3. Lifetime value. Don't view each new customer as a one-time sale. Remember, you will normally lose money on the first sale to a new client. The average business will need to sell to him two times before it begins to make a profit from him.

With this in mind, you need to focus on bringing the customer back on a regular basis. Therefore, any script campaign that covers its cost initially will turn out to be very profitable in the long term. A realistic response rate would be between 10–25 percent. Don't ever think in terms of response, though; it's largely irrelevant.

What Makes a Successful Script?

The actual specifics of how to write a great script are covered in the next section, but let's get a broad overview now.

It's important to take care of the big issues before worrying about little things like what the best word to use is. Here are the four main things to consider when planning a script:

Targeted Lists: You don't want to speak to anyone who would not be interested in your product or service.

Process: You need to plan your process. It's unlikely you'll sell large, expensive items in one step, and you're really kidding yourself if you can't close a $50 sale in two steps or less.

Urgency: People can put off buying forever. If you don't give them a reason to act now, your script will be unlikely to work.

You-Focus: Your script needs to be focused on the customers. If it says "I" and "we" throughout, it's likely to bore them, and you can't bore people into buying from you.

You need to say something like this: "So it sounds like *you* need this. By buying from us, *you* will get that plus a whole lot more, and I know that's important to *you*."

In short, a successful script is based on a successful idea. It doesn't matter which way you say something that's uninteresting, unappealing, and unaffordable—it'll still sounds like rubbish. Likewise, if you've got a great offer and product, and you've really targeted the market well, there's not much you can do to go wrong.

Give some thought to the overall picture first. Is what you're offering really worth the trouble of marketing it? Perhaps you might have to face the hard reality that the reason your business is not succeeding is simple—it's a bad business.

Remember, if your business seems impossible to market, perhaps it is. But by the same token, you'll never know until you try.

The Five Steps to Creating Powerful Scripts

Step 1: Who Is Your Target Market?

Before you put pen to paper, you need to identify exactly who it is you're trying to reach. Precisely who is your target market?

A failure to answer this question will cost you hundreds of wasted dollars and lead to a poor conversion rate. Imagine a company that sells skateboards telemarketing a retirement village. You need to know who your potential customers are before you begin writing, or using, your script.

Of course, it depends on the situation. It may be a cold telemarketing campaign, a phone-answering script, or a script for your customers in-store. Whatever type of script you use, you need to define who they are and what they want.

Knowing your target market will also enable you to speak in a way that your prospects will relate to. Using terms and phrases that are commonly used by them will greatly increase the effectiveness of your script.

So let's get specific. Who are the people most likely to be interested in your product or service? Here are some guidelines:

Age: How old are they? Don't just say "all ages" or "a variety of ages." We want to create a mental picture of your average customers. Think of an age that symbolizes most of them.

Sex: Are they male or female? Half and half is too broad. Practically every business is split one way or the other. Give it some real thought. Which gender does most business with you currently?

Income: How much do they make? Do they earn a great living or are they scraping for every dollar, always looking for deals? It's essential you find this out.

Where do they live? Are they local, or do they come from miles around to deal with you?

Education: How do they speak and what do they read? It's important to speak in the same way they do. Use the jargon they use and try to sound as if you're one of them.

Step 2: Where Do You Find a Suitable List of Prospects?

In most cases, finding a list is not the question—prospects may phone you directly, drop into your store, or come from another marketing strategy you are running.

If you are doing a cold telemarketing campaign, the issue of where you find a list becomes a big one. The wrong list will kill your campaign and drive your telemarketers to premature aging. The right list will make you rich.

There are basically three ways to obtain a list:

Buy one from a list broker. This is a quick, but expensive, way to get a list. Most brokers can provide you with lists that target particular geographic or demographic segments of the population. For example, you can buy one that will give you the names and addresses of women aged between 30 and 55, with an income of over $40,000 per year who live within a seven block radius of your store. While brokers can provide you with very specific lists, they tend to be far more expensive than general lists they've already compiled. Cost will normally dictate how targeted you can be when buying a list from these companies.

Use someone else's list. Find a noncompetitive company with a similar target market to your own. Then simply ask them if you could call their list. The success of this relies on your having a good relationship with the business in question. Although this method can be hit or miss, it can also be a very inexpensive way of reaching potential customers. To sweeten the deal, it may be worth offering the host business a commission or an incentive based on the number of products you sell.

Create your own. One way to compile your own list is to run a competition. To enter, people simply need to write their names and phone numbers on the entry form provided and then drop it in a box. By offering one of your products or services as the prize, you have a greater chance of reaching only those people who are genuinely interested in what you have to sell.

To set up this competition, you need to have tickets printed and a venue to run it in. Approach a shopping center, sporting club, or retail outlet to see if they'll let you leave your tickets and entry box on their premises. Alternatively, you can run it as a "cut-out-the-coupon" competition in the local paper. If the prize you offer is of a high enough dollar value, the paper may run it for you free of charge. Contact their promotions manager and explain your idea. You'll need to stress the interest the competition's going to create and how it will increase the paper's circulation.

Of course, you can also create a list by going through the White or Yellow Pages, or by purchasing a list from an approved broker. Bear in mind, these lists tend to be either completely untargeted, or used by every other business as well. But the right script, product, and offer can work well with almost any half-targeted list.

Step 3: What Do You Want to Say to Your Prospects?

There's often heated debate about which type of scripts work best, but there is never disagreement about which don't. Those are ones with no obvious purpose.

Your script needs to have a clear purpose; it needs to take people from Point A to Point B. What are those points? Point A is your initial statement. The rest of the script should lead to Point B, which is where you ask the prospect to act now—to commit.

Most important is understanding your customers. If you understand their needs, wants, and positions, you can sell almost anything to them.

Before writing anything, you need to decide exactly what you want your prospects to do on hearing your script. What is your Point B? Do you want them to present you with a credit card then and there, or to simply make an appointment?

Of course, there's different psychology behind each type of objective. To make a sale, you need to answer all their objections. To make an appointment, you simply have to suggest any objections they have can be answered, and will be addressed in detail further down the track.

Once you know what you want to achieve, you need to put yourself in their position. What do they already know about you? This is your Point A. How do they feel about you? How do they generally feel about your product or service? How often have people in your industry harassed them? Do they want to spend a lot of time or just get it over with? What objections do they have? What else is important?

Now, you have to determine the path from Point A to Point B—how can you lead people through the decision-making process?

We'll work that out next, but first, let's deal with something even more important.

It pays to remember that simply asking people to act now (or for that matter, *telling* them to act now) is rarely enough. You need to give them a good reason why *now* is the time to do something.

See, most purchases can be delayed forever. It's one thing to create desire, but it's another to actually get people to part with their cash. Every month, customers have to decide what to spend their money on. It could very realistically be a decision between buying your state-of-the-art DVD player, and buying the children clothes for winter.

Every buyer has priorities. Of course, there are ways of rearranging these priorities. If you offer a special deal on the DVD player, the customers may decide to buy it then, as they may not get it at that price again.

The question becomes, how do you offer a great deal without slicing your profit margin drastically? There are a couple of ways.

First, make sure you are selling products or services that have a high margin. Often, that's not possible—try getting a high margin on gasoline. If you have the option of gearing your business towards higher margin items, do so, as it'll make it much easier for you to come up with great deals later on.

If you can't do this, you need to find items or services that are highly valued by the customer, yet have a low cost. Extra service is an old standby. Information booklets are another. Even better are services you can get for free from other businesses. For example, a hairdresser could offer to introduce her clients to a spa, if the spa agrees to give every customer a free facial.

Of course, you can create urgency by placing a limitation on the availability of your offer. You could say these prices will be available only for the next two weeks until the new model arrives, or that prices are about to rise, or that you'll only be in town for the next four days. Naturally, being truthful is better—people are excellent at picking up insincerity.

Step 4: How Do You Write Your Script?

It's a common misconception that you have to be a great writer, or some wizard with words, to write a script that works. That's rubbish. People who know their market, and who know how to come up with a good offer, have written many of the most successful scripts. Their writing skills are irrelevant.

Simply calling a database of stressed-out executives with a script that says "100 percent less stress in 10 minutes or it's free—guaranteed," is probably enough. It doesn't matter what language you use, or even if you use words incorrectly. At the end of the day, who cares about the grammar? Of course, if your market is high school English teachers, you might want to think twice.

It might sound funny, but most people won't even know if you're using proper English or not. As long as your message is clear, quick, and well targeted, your script will work. It's much like drinking wine: If you drink a good wine from an ordinary glass, it'll taste just as good as it would from a crystal one. People may prefer it in a beautiful crystal glass, but if they had no choice, they'd drink it, and enjoy it, anyway.

There is only one sin you don't want to commit when writing a script, and that's getting off the point or rambling on too long. If every word and every sentence says something important for the sale, that's fine. If your script is full of nonsense, people will lose interest very quickly and hit you with the old standby—"I'm not interested!"

Each successful script follows a basic formula, although they do vary depending on the situation and their objective. Here are some guidelines for each type of script.

Telemarketing (Cold List)

Greeting: Include a greeting that announces your name, your company, and asks how the prospect is. It's essential you ask the obligatory "how are you" slowly, and take time listening to the response. If you seem to be rushing through this part, it'll set the tone for the rest of the script.

Outline Reason for Call: You must explain why you are calling, but always ask for permission. Say, "Is it OK if I outline the reason for my call today?" Then do exactly that. Explain the process you'll be running through, then ask: "Is it OK if we go through the call that way?" People tend to be a bit surprised by this approach, but that's a good thing. You want to stand out, giving the impression that this is something different, and that you're a professional.

Ask Open-Ended Questions: Without doubt, this is the most important thing anyone could ever learn about scripts. You must ask questions that can't be answered with a straight "yes" or "no." It's a good idea to ask questions that encourage the prospects to do the selling for you. Tell them how good you are, then ask this: "And what benefits can you see in having a business that will do all that for you?" It's a tricky way to get them to say, "Yes, it would be a good idea to deal with you."

Get Agreement: At some point, you must get some feedback from the prospects. The best way is to ask a rhetorical question, then get them to answer with a "yes." This is the one time you break the rules. You say, "So it sounds like you'd benefit by [benefit 1], [benefit 2], and [benefit 3]—that sounds pretty irresistible, doesn't it?" Or what about, "It seems like you'd be crazy to stay with your current supplier, doesn't it?" Or, as a softer approach, what about, "You can see the sense in what I'm saying, can't you?" Once you have their agreement on this, there is no reason why the process shouldn't proceed to Point B—your objective.

Deal with Objections: At some point, your prospects will probably raise some objections. That's fine—as long as you know how to deal with them. The first thing you say is, "Can you elaborate on that for me?" Get them talking a bit more. Then say something like, "Now, assuming I could show you a way to get around that problem, would you be interested in that information?" Then answer the objection, but do it empathetically—that is, say: "I understand that, and I used to think that way myself, but then I discovered. . . ." Or alternately, "Yes, I know what you mean. Someone else said that to me recently, but here's something that will surprise you." Then, it's really up to you. You need to determine the major objections and a way to acknowledge them before turning them around. If people say, "I haven't got the money," you could respond, "I understand that. It's usually short this time of year. But there's some good news—you can afford this. We have layaway, payment plans, and interest-free financing for six months. We also accept all major credit cards. Which of those would be most suitable for you?" If they say, "I don't have time," you could counter with this: "Yes, it's hard to find time when life is so busy. But you know what, it only takes one hour a week, and the benefits are tremendous. Wouldn't you say it's worth investing just one hour in yourself? You know, doing something just for *you?*" Of course, there'll be times when you run into objections that can't be answered. If you offer your best payment plans and they still can't afford it, then forget it. If they've just bought a competitor's brand and would never change, forget it too. These people aren't in your target market, and should be scratched from your list. Remember, you can't sell to people who don't have the means to buy, or no interest in doing so.

Close and Take the Next Step: If you've gotten this far, you should be able to assume the person is interested in buying. If you have agreement and you've dealt with their objections, it's time to nail it down. The first thing to do is try an assumptive close. "We'll make an appointment now—

would you prefer tomorrow or Thursday?" Or, "OK, which credit card is it easiest to process that on?" Something else to consider is making the decision for them. Instead of saying, "Would you like to book your appointment now?" why not say, "I'd like to book you in for your appointment now—would today or tomorrow suit you better?" If your close fails and they say no, not yet, or they don't want to, say, "OK, I thought you were ready to get the process underway. Level with me— what's preventing you from making this decision right now?" You could also ask, "What is it you're not telling me?"

Telemarketing (Follow-up on Direct Mail)

Greeting: Include a greeting that announces your name, your company, and asks how the prospect is. It's essential you ask the obligatory "how are you" slowly and take time listening to the response. If you seem to be rushing through that part, it'll set the tone for the entire script.

Outline Reason for Call: You must explain why you are calling, but always ask for permission. Say, "Is it OK if I outline the reason for my call today?" Then do exactly that. Explain the process you'll be running through, then ask: "Is it OK if we go through the call that way?" People tend to be a bit surprised by this approach, but that's a good thing. You want to stand out, giving the impression that this is something different, and that you're a professional.

Allude to the Letter: The beauty of sending a letter first is that it gives you an excuse to call. You can say, "I sent you a letter last week and promised to give you a call about now. You may remember the letter—the headline was [headline]." Then ask, "Do you remember the letter I'm talking about?" Whether they say "yes" or "no" doesn't matter. If they say "yes," you can say, "Great, I just wanted to run through the main points and discuss the offer I made in that letter." If they say "no," say, "That's fine, I'll give you the gist of it now, and save you time reading it later." It's a good idea to include some gimmick with your letter, so it gets remembered.

Ask Open-Ended Questions: You must ask questions that can't be answered with a straight "yes" or "no." It's a good idea to ask questions that encourage the prospects to do the selling for you. Tell them how good you are, then ask this: "And what benefits can you see in having a business that will do all that for you?" It's a tricky way to get them to say, "Yes, it would be a good idea to deal with you."

Get Agreement: At some point, you must get some feedback from the prospects. The best way is to ask a rhetorical question, and get them to answer with a "yes." This is the one time you break the rules. You say, "So it sounds like you'd benefit by [benefit 1], [benefit 2], and [benefit 3]—that sounds pretty irresistible, doesn't it?" Or what about, "It seems like you'd be crazy to stay with your current supplier, doesn't it?" Or, as a softer approach, what about, "You can see the sense in what I'm saying, can't you?" Once you have their agreement on this, there is no reason why the process shouldn't proceed to Point B—your objective.

Deal with Objections: At some point, your prospects will probably raise some objections. That's fine—as long as you know how to deal with them. The first thing you say is, "Can you elaborate on that for me?" Get them talking a bit more. Then say something like, "Now, assuming I could show you a way to get around that problem, would you be interested in that information?" Then answer the objection, but do it empathetically—that is, say, "I understand that, and I used to think that way myself, but then I discovered. . . ." Or alternately, "Yes, I know what you mean. Someone else said that to me recently, but here's something that will surprise you." Then, it's really up to you. You need to determine the major objections and a way to acknowledge them before turning them around. If people say, "I haven't got the money," you could respond, "I understand that. It's usually short this time of year. But there's some good news—you can afford this. We have layaway, payment plans, and interest-free financing for six months. We also accept all major credit cards. Which of those would be most suitable for you?" If they say, "I don't have time," you could counter with this: "Yes, it's hard to find time when life is so busy. But you know what, it only takes one hour a week, and the benefits are tremendous. Wouldn't you say it's worth investing just one hour in yourself? You know, doing something just for *you?*" Of course, there'll be times when you run into objections that can't be answered. If you offer your best payment plans and they still can't afford it, then forget it. If they've just bought a competitor's brand and would never change, forget it too. These people aren't in your target market, and should be scratched from your list. Remember, you can't sell to people who don't have the means to buy, or no interest in doing so.

Close and Take the Next Step: If you've gotten this far, you should be able to assume the people are interested in buying. If you have agreement and you've dealt with their objections, it's time to nail it down. The first thing to do is try an assumptive close. "We'll make an appointment now—would you prefer tomorrow or Thursday?" Or, "OK, which credit card is it easiest to process that on?" Something else to consider is making the decision for them. Instead of saying, "Would you like to book your appointment now?" why not say, "I'd like to book you in for your appointment now—would today or tomorrow suit you better?" If your close fails and they say no, not yet, or they don't want to, say, "OK, I thought you were ready to get the process underway. Level with me—what's preventing you from making this decision right now?" You could also ask, "What is it you're not telling me?"

Door-to-Door (Cold)

Get a Human Element Up Front: There's no reason you can't run through the first minute or two without even telling them who you are. If you have a name-badge and a clipboard, they'll know you've come about something. Why not say, "Geez, that's a huge dog you've got—I bet he could swallow a man whole." Or, "Man, this weather's driving me crazy. Just when you think it's going to clear up, it starts raining again. I've been soaked four times, you know what I mean?" Once you've built this kind of simple relationship, people are more likely to hear you out.

Greeting: Include a greeting that announces your name, your company, and asks how the prospect is. It's essential you ask the obligatory "how are you" slowly and take time listening to the response. If you seem to be rushing through that part, it'll set the tone for the entire script.

Outline Reason for Visit: You must explain why you are visiting, but always ask for permission. Say, "Is it OK if I outline the reason for my visit today?" Then do exactly that. Explain the process you'll be running through, then ask: "Is it OK if we go through the visit that way?" People tend to be a bit surprised by this approach, but that's a good thing. You want to stand out, giving the impression that this is something different, and that you're a professional.

Ask Open-Ended Questions: You must ask questions that can't be answered with a straight "yes" or "no." It's a good idea to ask questions that encourage the prospects to do the selling for you. Tell them how good you are, then ask this: "And what benefits can you see in having a business that will do all that for you?" It's a tricky way to get them to say, "Yes, it would be a good idea to deal with you."

Get Inside: This is more important for some types of businesses than others. An easy way to do this is to say, "Look, it might be better if I explain this inside." Don't say, "Would that be OK?" Just say it as it's written. People will feel they're being very rude if they say, "Well, buzz off then," although some will anyway. Another approach is, "It sounds like this could be perfect for you—can we discuss it over a cup of tea?"

Get Agreement: At some point, you must get some feedback from the prospects. The best way is to ask a rhetorical question, and get them to answer with a "yes." This is the one time you break the rules. You say, "So it sounds like you'd benefit by [benefit 1], [benefit 2], and [benefit 3]—that sounds pretty irresistible doesn't it?" Or what about, "It seems like you'd be crazy to stay with your current supplier, doesn't it?" Or, as a softer approach, what about, "You can see the sense in what I'm saying, can't you?" Once you have their agreement on this, there is no reason why the process shouldn't proceed to Point B—your objective.

Deal with Objections: At some point, the prospects will probably raise some objections. That's fine—as long as you know how to deal with them. The first thing you say is, "Can you elaborate on that for me?" Get them talking a bit more. Then say something like, "Now, assuming I could show you a way to get around that problem, would you be interested in that information?" Then answer the objection, but do it empathetically—that is, say, "I understand that, and I used to think that way myself, but then I discovered. . . ." Or alternately, "Yes, I know what you mean. Someone else said that to me recently, but here's something that will surprise you." Then, it's really up to you. You need to determine the major objections and a way to acknowledge them before turning them around. If someone says, "I haven't got the money," you could respond, "I understand that. It's usually short this time of year. But there's some good news—you can afford this. We have layaway, payment plans, and interest-free financing for six months. We also accept all major credit cards. Which of those would be most suitable for you?" If they say, "I don't have time," you could counter with this: "Yes, it's hard to find time when life is so busy. But you know what, it only takes one hour a week, and the benefits are huge. Wouldn't you say it's worth investing just one hour in yourself? You know, doing something just for *you?*" Of course, there'll be times when you run into objections that can't be answered. If you offer your best payment plans and they still can't afford it, then forget it. If they've just bought a competitor's brand and would never change, forget it too. These people aren't in your target market, and should be scratched from your list. Remember, you can't sell to people who don't have the means to buy, or no interest in doing so.

Close and Take the Next Step: If you've gotten this far, you should be able to assume that the people are interested in buying. If you have agreement and you've dealt with their objections, it's time to nail it down. The first thing to do is try an assumptive close. "We'll make an appointment now—would you prefer tomorrow or Thursday?" Or, "OK, which credit card is it easiest to process that on?" Something else to consider is making the decision for them. Instead of saying, "Would you like to book your appointment now?" why not say, "I'd like to book you in for your appointment now—would today or tomorrow suit you better?" If your close fails and they say no, not yet, or they don't want to, say, "OK, I thought you were ready to get the process underway. Level with me— what's preventing you from making this decision right now?" You could also ask, "What is it you're not telling me?"

Incoming Phone Script (Inquiry)

Greeting: Include a greeting that announces your name, your company, then thanks the prospect for calling. Say, "Hi, thanks for calling [business name]. This is [your full name]." Slow down with this part. If you seem to be rushing through, it'll set the tone for the entire call.

Get into the Questions: Whatever question your prospects ask first, make sure you say, "Thanks for your call. Just so I can help you best, is it OK if I ask you a couple of questions?" Don't, under any circumstances, answer their initial question.

Ask Open-Ended Questions: You must ask questions that can't be answered with a straight "yes" or "no." It's a good idea to ask questions that encourage the prospects to do the selling for you. Ask them specifically what they need, who else they've seen, how much they think is a fair price to pay, etc. Then tell them how good you are, and ask this: "What benefits can you see in having a business that will do all that for you?" It's a tricky way to get them to say, "Yes, it would be a good idea to deal with you."

Get Agreement: At some point, you must get some feedback from your prospects. The best way is to ask a rhetorical question, and get them to answer with a "yes." This is the one time you break the rules. You say, "So it sounds like you'd benefit by [benefit 1], [benefit 2], and [benefit 3]—that sounds pretty irresistible doesn't it?" Or what about, "It seems like you'd be crazy to stay with your current supplier, doesn't it?" Or, as a softer approach, what about, "You can see the sense in what I'm saying, can't you?" Once you have their agreement on this, there is no reason why the process shouldn't proceed to Point B—your objective.

Deal with Objections: At some point, the prospect will probably raise some objections. That's fine—as long as you know how to deal with them. The first thing you say is, "Can you elaborate on that for me?" Get them talking a bit more. Then say something like, "Now, assuming I could show you a way to get around that problem, would you be interested in that information?" Then answer the objection, but do it empathetically—that is, say, "I understand that, and I used to think that way myself, but then I discovered. . . ." Or alternately, "Yes, I know what you mean. Someone else said that to me recently, but here's something that will surprise you." Then, it's really up to you. You need to determine the major objections and a way to acknowledge them before turning them around. If someone says, "I haven't got the money," you could respond, "I understand that. It's usually short this time of year. But there's some good news—you can afford this. We have layaway, payment plans, and interest-free financng for six months. We also accept all major credit cards. Which of those would be most suitable for you?" If they say, "I don't have time," you could counter with this: "Yes, it's hard to find time when life is so busy. But you know what, it only takes one hour a week, and the benefits are tremendous. Wouldn't you say it's worth investing just one hour in yourself? You know, doing something just for *you?*" Of course, there'll be times when you run into objections that can't be answered. If you offer your best payment plans and they still can't afford it, then forget it. If they've just bought a competitor's brand and would never change, forget it too. These people aren't in your target market, and should be scratched from your list. Remember, you can't sell to people who don't have the means to buy, or no interest in doing so.

Close and Take the Next Step: If you've gotten this far, you should be able to assume that the people are interested in buying. If you have agreement and you've dealt with their objections, it's time to nail it down. The first thing to do is trial an assumptive close. "We'll make an appointment now—would you prefer tomorrow or Thursday?" Or, "OK, which credit card is it easiest to process that on?" Something else to consider is making the decision for them. Instead of saying, "Would you like to book in for your appointment now?" why not say, "I'd like to book your appointment now—would today or tomorrow suit you better?" If your close fails and they say "no," not yet, or they don't want to, say, "OK, I thought you were ready to get the process underway. Level with me— what's preventing you from making this decision right now?" You could also ask, "What is it you're not telling me?"

In-Store Script

Greeting: When people come in, say, "Hi, have you been in before?" Slow down with this part. If you seem to be rushing through, it'll set the tone for the entire visit. If they say "no," say, "Great, thanks for coming in. Let me show you around." If they say "yes," say, "I thought so—you look familiar. What brings you back today?"

Ask Open-Ended Questions: You must ask questions that can't be answered with a straight "yes" or "no." It's a good idea to ask questions that encourage the prospects to do the selling for you. Ask them specifically what they need, who else they've seen, how much they think is a fair price to pay, etc. Then tell them how good you are, then ask this: "And what benefits can you see in having a business that will do all that for you?" It's a tricky way to get them to say, "Yes, it would be a good idea to deal with you."

Get Agreement: At some point, you must get some feedback from the prospects. The best way is to ask a rhetorical question, and get them to answer with a "yes." This is the one time you break the rules. You say, "So it sounds like you'd benefit by [benefit 1], [benefit 2], and [benefit 3]—that sounds pretty irresistible doesn't it?" Or what about, "It seems like you'd be crazy to stay with your current supplier, doesn't it?" Or, as a softer approach, what about, "You can see the sense in what I'm saying, can't you?" Once you have their agreement on this, there is no reason why the process shouldn't proceed to Point B—your objective.

Deal with Objections: At some point, your prospects will probably raise some objections. That's fine—as long as you know how to deal with them. The first thing you say is, "Can you elaborate on that for me?" Get them talking a bit more. Then say something like, "Now, assuming I could show you a way to get around that problem, would you be interested in that information?" Then answer the objection, but do it empathetically—that is, say, "I understand that, and I used to think that way myself, but then I discovered. . . ." Or alternately, "Yes, I know what you mean. Someone else said that to me recently, but here's something that will surprise you." Then, it's really up to you. You need to determine the major objections and a way to acknowledge them before turning them around. If people say, "I haven't got the money," you could respond, "I understand that. It's usually short this time of year. But there's some good news—you can afford this. We have layaway, payment plans, and interest-free financing for six months. We also accept all major credit cards. Which of those would be most suitable for you?" If they say, "I don't have time," you could counter with this: "Yes, it's hard to find time when life is so busy. But you know what, it only takes one hour a week, and the benefits are huge. Wouldn't you say it's worth investing just one hour in yourself? You know, doing something just for *you?*" Of course, there'll be times when you run into objections that can't be answered. If you offer your best payment plans and they still can't afford it, then forget it. If they've just bought a competitor's brand and would never change, forget it too. These people aren't in your target market, and should be scratched from your list. Remember, you can't sell to people who don't have the means to buy, or no interest in doing so.

Close and Take the Next Step: If you've gotten this far, you should be able to assume that the people are interested in buying. If you have agreement and you've dealt with their objections, it's time to nail it down. The first thing to do is trial an assumptive close. "We'll make an appointment now—would you prefer tomorrow or Thursday?" Or, "OK, which credit card is it easiest to process that on?" Something else to consider is making the decision for them. Instead of saying, "Would you like to book your appointment now?" why not say, "I'd like to book you in for your appointment now—would today or tomorrow suit you better?" If your close fails and they say "no," not yet, or they don't want to, say, "OK, I thought you were ready to get the process underway. Level with me—what's preventing you from making this decision right now?" You could also ask, "What is it you're not telling me?"

Step 5: What Else Do You Need to Think About?

Use this section as a final checklist. Once you're happy with the script, run through and make sure you're ready to get started. Here are a few things you may not have thought about:

Team Training: Do your team members fully understand the script that you've implemented? It's important they understand the vital role they are to play in this strategy. If your new customers come in and find your team uninterested in providing them with tip-top service, the exercise will be a waste of time. Your team also need to be shown how to use the script, and they'll need *lots* of practice. It'll represent a new way of going about their jobs, so give them time to adjust.

Check Stock and Team Levels: It's unlikely your script will make hundreds of sales all at once (very few actually do), but you need to be prepared for a sizable response. There would be nothing worse than having a rush of new sales, only to find you have no stock or are too busy to fill the orders. Plan for your script campaign by making sure you can cater to any increased demand.

"OK, Charlie, now it's your turn. See if you can write a script for an incoming call. And remember, it must be a script that any one of your team members can use."

"But I'm the only one who answers the phone."

"What if you're sick, or out at the bank?"

"Then my wife comes in. She takes messages."

"This is clearly an area you need to work on, Charlie. You see, my experience is that people don't want to keep phoning back. They want to get it sorted out then and there. By not being able to help them on the spot, you're probably losing business. This is where scripts come in. Your employees can then handle calls, as long as they stick to the script. So, with that in mind, let's see what you come up with."

"No worries, Brad. Here goes…"

Charlie's Incoming Script

Introduction.

Good morning/afternoon. Thanks for calling Charlie's Garage. This is [name].

[Customer question]

Thanks for your call. Just so I can help you best, is it OK if I ask you a few questions?

[Sure]

Great. First, have you had your car serviced here before?

[Yes/no]

IF YES.

What did you find when you were here last? Were you happy with the price, quality of workmanship, and service?

[Explanation]

Right, it looks like I can help you out there. We [explain benefits]. And to make sure you avoid that problem again, we also [explain what you do differently]. By the way, can I just ask what you'll be using this [x] for?

[Answer]

OK, that sounds interesting. I can think of four different types of [x] that would suit that perfectly. You really need to take a look, though. I could see you this afternoon, or tomorrow morning—which of those would suit you best?

IF NO.

OK, how many places have you seen so far?

[Number]

Right. Has anyone told you about the different types of [x]?

[Yes/no]

Uh huh. I see. There are two other things I'd mention. The first is [fact 1], the second, and this is what most places don't seem to mention, is that [fact 2]. By the way, can I just ask what you'll be using this [x] for?

[Answer]

OK, that sounds interesting. I can think of four different types of [x] that would suit that perfectly. You really need to take a look, though. I could see you this afternoon, or tomorrow morning—which of those would suit you best?

End.

All right, I've got that down on my calendar for [rough time, e.g. midafternoon]. By the way, your name is. . .?

That's great [name]. I look forward to seeing you then. Bye for now.

If they ask: "What's the price?"

OK, that depends. First, are you interested in getting away as cheaply as possible, or is quality more important?

[They'll probably answer, "A bit of both."]

Right, because there is some really cheap and poor quality stuff available. I have some of it, but I usually reserve it for people who don't care about the end result. Could I just ask, have you been quoted prices anywhere else?

[Answer]

If you don't mind my asking, what did they quote you?

[Answer]

If it's super cheap.

That sounds a bit like one of those cheap and poorly made products. I can match that, but for what you're looking to do, I'd recommend [x]—it's only $[x] more and will do a 200 percent better job. Or if you're after top quality stuff, go for [y]—it's incredible. My professional customers use that. I've got both of them in stock. I could show them to you this afternoon or tomorrow morning. Which suits you best?

If it's expensive.

Wow, that's surprising. I always thought those guys were cheap. They might have put their prices up. I can do that same product for less than that. But I'd recommend [x]. It's not as cheap, but it'll do the job 200 percent better. It'll probably work out to less than what they've quoted you. Or, if you want to get away from rock bottom, try [y]—it's great value. I've got both of those in stock. I could show them to you this afternoon or tomorrow morning. Which of those suits you best?

If it's in the middle.

I can match that, but for what you're looking to do, I'd recommend [x]—it's only $[x] more and will do a 200 percent better job. Or if you're after top quality stuff, go for [y]—it's incredible. My professional customers use that. I've got both in stock. I could show them to you this afternoon or tomorrow morning. Which suits you best?

"Will that do, Brad?"

That's great, Charlie. Now write one for something more specific. Let's say someone calls in about a set of new tires. Can you do that?"

"Yes. Here goes."

Charlie's Script for Incoming Calls on Tires

Greeting

Good morning/afternoon. Thanks for calling Charlie's Garage. This is Charlie.

[Just calling about the. . ., What's the price on. . .]

Thanks for your call. Could I just ask your name?

[John]

Thanks John. Just so I can help you best, would it be OK if I asked you a few questions?

[Sure]

Questions

Great. First, what sort of vehicle do you own?

[Falcon]

I see, and when was the last time you had your tires replaced?

Path 1

[six months ago]

Right, they didn't last long. What brand were they?

[X brand]

Yep, the cheapies. You'll find they wear out pretty quickly. For your car I'd recommend [y] brand. They'll last twice as long, give you a better ride, and only cost a couple of dollars more.

Path 2

[18 months]

Right, and you've been happy with them?

[Yes]

Great. I've got those in stock and I'll fit them for you today.

OR

[NO]

I've got a brand that is just slightly better than the previous tires you've used. Plus, they cost a little less and I can fit those for you today.

End

How many tires do you need?

[number]

Great. I could do that for you at 12:00 p.m. or later; say 4:30 p.m. Which suits you best?

[time]

Excellent. And your full name is. . .?

[John Market]

And your best contact number there. . .?

[number]

Right, John, I'll see you at [time]. It'll take about 15 minutes. I'll prepare a cup of coffee for you while you wait. How do you have it?

[Milk and one sugar]

Great. And could I just ask, do you prefer chocolate or blueberry muffins?

[Chocolate]

OK, I'll see you soon.

Examples

This next section includes some great examples of tried and tested scripts that work. Try them for yourself or adapt them to suit your own particular situation.

Door-to-Door

Hi there. I'm Jim Murray from Pure Water Systems. How are you today? Great. Would it be OK if I explained the reason for my visit today?

Thanks.

Pure Water Systems, the company I work for, is offering 12 homeowners in this area a free five-day trial of these new Benchtop Water Filters. We're guaranteeing you'll be thrilled with the difference in the taste of your water. If not, we take the unit back and ask for no payment. Can I just ask, have you ever had a water filter before?

Right.

You may not know it, but water filters are now so good that they produce water that tastes better than the stuff you buy. Most people find that hard to believe, so I offer a taste test. I've got a sample of water straight out of the tap, and a sample that's been filtered. Which would you like to taste first?

OK, here you go. What do you think?

Now, try the other one. Notice a difference?

Excellent. Now, as we only have a limited number of filters to offer for trial, I need to run you through three qualification questions. As I'm sure you can understand, we need to make sure these trial units go to the right people. Is it OK if I run through those three questions now?

Great. Did you know your body needs about eight glasses of water a day to function properly?

Uh-huh. Second, did you know that unfiltered tap water can contain harmful chemicals?

Right. And lastly, do you ever choose other drinks over water because of the poor taste of tap water?

Hmmm. Interesting. I think you'd benefit from trying our water filter. The installation just takes a couple of minutes. Is it OK if I do that now?

Great.

Thanks for your time today. I'll phone you in five days to ask whether you and your family have noticed a difference. Could I just take down your name? And your phone number?

Thanks. Here's some more information on our water filters. It's just a one-page sheet that outlines the benefits of drinking filtered water.

I'll give you a call soon.

Bye for now.

Follow-up Script

Hi [name]. It's Jim from Pure Water Systems. You've been living with our trial water filter for five days now. How are you?

That's great. What have been the main benefits you've found using our water filter?

Right, and has your whole family noticed the difference?

Uh-huh. Do they seem to be drinking more water?

Excellent. [name], do you like the bench top style, or would you prefer one under your sink that can't be seen?

I see. We're actually running a special on those right now. The normal price is [$x]. We have six brand new units we're running out at [$y]. How does that fit with what you had in mind?

Great. I could arrange delivery and free installation on Tuesday morning or Wednesday evening. Which of those suits you best?

Excellent. Now which credit card is it easiest to process that on?

And the number is. . .

OR

OK, would it be all right if I picked up a check when we install the unit?

Great. I've got that down in my appointment book. I'll see you then.

Telemarketing Script

Greeting

Hi there, could I speak to Mr. or Mrs. X?

Thanks. Hi. My name's [name] and I'm from a company called Sprayseal. How are you tonight?

Explanation

Great. Can I just outline the reason for my call?

Thanks. As I said, I'm with a company called Sprayseal. We're scheduled to do two appointments in [street] tomorrow, and a couple over the next week. We're out there inspecting roofs, checking for leaks, corrosion and other common problems in your area. By the way, what type of roof do you have?

Questions

I see. Do you know how old it is?

Mmmm, it's getting old. We find roofs need to be checked every couple of years otherwise they develop leaks, which let the water in. They rust and discolor which, simply looks bad and devalues your home. Could I just ask, when was the last time you had your roof professionally checked?

Really? [with some surprise] What problems have you noticed? Roof leaks, for example?

For Tiles

Cracked tiles, fading tiles, cracked mortar, or cracked ridging? What about loose tiles?

For Iron

How about discoloration and rust? Loose nails, lifting sheets, flaky and/or oxidizing paint?

For Fibro

Black and moldy roof? Sheets have become porous? Do you know about the asbestos risks with Fibro roofs?

End

Listen, I can book you for a free roof inspection. We're going to be out there anyway, and it only takes 15 to 30 minutes. Our guys are professionals—they'll get up there and do a complete examination. If there's nothing wrong, they'll let you know. If there is something to look at, they'll also tell you. It's completely free. I know if it was me, I'd have it done. If you don't take care of the little things early on, they get bigger, and much more expensive later on. It's worth a look. Now what's a time when both you and your partner will be home? Does tomorrow suit you both, or would you prefer Thursday?

Great. Morning or afternoon?

OK, and would you prefer 10:00 a.m. or 11:30 a.m.?

That's fantastic. Oh, one more thing—your first name is. . .?

OK [name]. Our inspector, Harry, will come out and see you and your partner then.

Door-to-Door Script

Hi. My name's [full name]. I'm with a new business in the area called Enviro-friendly. We're just starting off and I wanted to say "hi" personally rather than just sending you a letter or flyer to add to your junk mail pile—you know what I mean?

Would it be OK if I outlined the purpose of my visit today?

First, I'd like to talk with you about the serious drainage problems residents in this area are experiencing. Many are experiencing blockages, bad smells, and other problems.

Second, I would like to offer you a quick, free check of your drains just to highlight where the problems might arise.

Third, given we can both see the benefit of keeping your drains problem- and smell-free from now on, I'd like to show you exactly how you could do that.

Would it be OK if I went through the visit this way?

Great. Could I just ask what sort of problems you may have experienced with your drains in the past, or that you know other people in the area have experienced?

What do you know about drains and drainage problems?

How did you fix it?

Was that expensive?

Has any company ever come to you and offered assistance with your drains?

Based on what you have just told me, it sounds like you are aware of drainage problems. However, you don't have a simple and effective way to clean and fix the problems. Is that right?

Let's have a look at your drains now and apply the *free* 15-point drainage inspection. [Check out drains]

Yeah, this is typical of what we've seen around here—you know, in some cases people have had to get their whole drainage system replaced because of problems with their drains. Servicing and replacements can cost anywhere from [$] to around [$]. Not a pretty situation. However, there is a way you can ensure you never again experience bad smells or blockages of any kind. Would it be OK if I go through how you do this now?

[Run through the demonstration with Drainsolv]

You obviously see the benefit of keeping your drains this way from now on?

Great. To achieve this, would it be OK if I just outlined the steps involved in getting this process under way?

First, we supply to you, at cost, one month's supply of the product. Consider it a trial. If it doesn't do precisely what I've promised it would, just send it back and we'll refund your money.

And by the way, the investment in the product is *only* $3 a week—so that's only $12 for the first month's supply. How does that fit with what you have in mind?

Great. Would you like to pay for that by credit card or would you like to make a out check for it now—which one suits you best?

Templates

We're now going to focus on how to write scripts. Work through the easy-to-follow steps and you'll have a series of templates to cater to any situation. Not only are they extremely effective and easy to use, they'll give your business a head start over your opposition.

How to Write a Direct Mail Follow-up Script

Step 1

Ensure you are smiling before you dial the number. A good technique is to picture the callers sitting on the other end of the line with their wallets open.

Step 2

Greet them and build rapport. It's important to sound like a breath of fresh air. Work yourself into a persona—one of friendliness and happiness. Say, "Hi [their first name]. How are today?" Take your time with this part of the call, and be genuinely interested in the answer. If you treat them like people, and not just a name on a page, you're likely to get a warmer response.

Step 3

Ask for permission. This is critical, as it gives you talking space and the permission to discuss whatever you have to discuss. Say, "Would it be OK if I outlined the reason for my call?" Alternately, try this: "Can I tell you why I'm calling today?" Or how about this: "Is it all right if I just cut right to the chase and tell you why I've phoned you today?"

Step 4

Outline the call. Explain precisely what you're going to say. For example, "First, I'm calling to check if you received a letter I personally addressed to you recently.

You may remember it—the letter with the [any gimmicks or special implements that are included in the letter]. Second, I wanted to talk to you about the offer I made in that letter. Third, given that you like what you hear, we'll discuss how you can take advantage of that offer."

Make sure you go through these points slowly. *Don't* just read them off as fast as you can. Ensure that the person on the other end is listening and understanding what you have to say.

Then say, "Would it be OK if I went through the call that way?" They should answer, "Yes."

If they say anything else, say, "Could I just ask why?" If they say, "I'm too busy," you reply, "That's fine, I understand. I do have something good to share with you, so I'll make a note to phone you back. I could do that later this afternoon, or tomorrow morning. Which of those is better for you?" If they say, "Neither," you say, "OK, give me a day and a time this week, and I'll work around that."

Step 5

Confirm they've received the letter. "Great [name]. Do you remember the letter I'm talking about? You may remember it contained a [special or unique inclusion]." Or, "You may remember that it talked about [key points in the letter]." If they say, "Yes, I remember," go on to the next point. If they say, "Not sure," or "No," you say, "That's fine. I can save you a lot of time by just outlining the key points with you now."

Step 6

Outline the key points in the letter. Say, "The letter talked about how you can [key benefit], and how my organization, [your business name], can help." Then lead into some specific questions about their business. Start with, "Can I just ask, what benefit do you see in [key benefit]?" Then continue with a list of open-ended questions, beginning with *what, how, when,* etc. Don't ask questions that may be answered with a straight "yes" or "no."

Some examples of questions:

"What have been your experiences with buying [your type of product]?"

"How would you rate your happiness with the businesses you've dealt with in the past?"

"When were you thinking about upgrading next?"

"How often do you need [your type of product]?"

"Have you had trouble with [key frustration]?"

"Do you see a benefit in getting around that?"

Next, you need to ask a key question. A good example is, "OK, so what's most important to you when buying [your type of product or service]?"

Then say, "Can you elaborate on that for me?" When you have an excellent outline of their current situation and needs, move on to the next step.

Step 7

Refer back to the offer. Say, "That's great, because we can really help you with that. You'll notice our letter contained an offer of [outline offer]. That means you'll get better service and a great deal to boot. How does that fit with what you have in mind?"

If the answer is, "Sounds good," or something similar, move onto the next step.

If not, say, "OK, which parts are you unsure about?" Or, "OK, what do we need to change to make it fit with what you had in mind?"

Then say, "OK, supposing I can give you [anything else they want], how does that fit with what you had in mind?" If they say, "Fine," then continue, "Great, because I can give you [explain an alternative solution that suits better]."

Step 8

Book an appointment, or make the sale direct. It pays to assume that the prospects are interested enough to want to see you, or to buy right now. And considering you have proposed an ideal solution to a problem they have, there is no reason why they wouldn't want to. Use the line, "That's great. It sounds as though we have what you're after. Assuming you're happy with what we've discussed, I could see you this afternoon at [time] or tomorrow morning at

[time]. Which of those suits you best?" Or, "Assuming you're happy with that, I could get that mailed to you today. What's your best delivery address?" Then say, "Great, and which credit card is it easiest to process that on?"

Step 9

Confirm. Say, "Excellent. It's been great to talk to you. And just for my records, is this the best number to get you on, or is there another line that suits you better?" Last, end on a high note. "Thanks so much for your call, and I look forward to seeing you at [appointment time]. Bye for now." Or, "Great. I'm just putting that in the mail for you now. I'll phone soon to check how it's going. Bye for now."

How to Write an Incoming Phone Script

Step 1

Wait for the phone to ring twice, and then answer it. Sooner than two rings makes the caller feel uncomfortable. More than two rings sounds unfriendly.

Step 2

Ensure you are smiling before you answer the phone. A good technique is to picture the callers sitting on the other end of the line with their wallets open.

Step 3

Your first line should be, "Good [morning/afternoon/evening]. Thanks for calling [your business name]. This is [your full name]." If they give you their name immediately, write it down.

Step 4

They will ask their first question at this point. Some common questions are, "Do you have any [x]?" or "What's the price on [x]?" Unless the question is something similar to, "Where do I mail the check to?" you *must* say, "Thanks for your call. Just so I can help you best, would it be OK if I asked a couple of questions?"

Step 5

Upon receiving their approval, begin asking open-ended questions. These are questions that start with *what, how, when,* etc. Questions that lead into a "yes" or "no" response will stop the flow of conversation. Here are some ideas on questions you could ask:

"Right. When do you need that [x]?"

"What have been your past experiences with [x]?"

"Why do you need an [x] right now?"

"So what are you looking for in an [x]?"

"How many quotes have you had on [x]?"

Each question builds a relationship with the prospects, and leads to the ultimate outcome—a clear picture of their wants, concerns, and attitudes. Also, it pays to ask, "Where did you hear about us?" and "What is it about the advertisement that made you want to phone?"

Step 6

Confirm that they are ready to make the decision. Ask, "Who else is involved in making this decision?" Also ask, "What is the most important thing you're looking for, with regard to [x]?"

Step 7

Offer a solution. Say, "Based on what you've told me, it sounds like [repeat their criteria for buying back to them]. With that in mind, I recommend the [best solution, with an explanation of why it is the ideal way to go]."

Step 8

Use a "temperature-checking" line. The ideal phrase is, "How does that fit with what you had in mind?"

If the answer is, "Sounds good," or something similar, move on to the next step.

If not, say, "OK. Which parts are you unsure about?" Or, "OK. What do we need to change to make it fit with what you had in mind?"

Then say, "OK. Supposing I can give you [anything else they want], how does that fit with what you had in mind?" If they say, "Fine," then say, "Great, because I can give you [explain an alternative solution that suits better]."

Step 9

Book an appointment. It pays to assume that the prospects are interested enough to want to come and see you. And considering you have proposed an ideal solution, there is no reason why they wouldn't want to. Use the line, "That's great. It sounds as though we have just what you're after. Assuming that you're happy with what we've discussed, I could see you this afternoon at [time] or tomorrow morning at [time]. Which of those suits you best?"

Step 10

Confirm. Say, "Excellent. I'm looking forward to it. Oh, by the way, what's your first name? Great [name], and your second name is. . .? Thanks, will anyone else be coming with you? What's their name? And just in case we need to reschedule, your phone number is?"

Last, end on a high note—"Thanks so much for your call. I look forward to seeing you at [appointment time]. Bye for now."

How to Write a Cold Telemarketing Script

Step 1

Ensure that you are smiling before you dial the number. A good technique is to picture the callers sitting on the other end of the line with their wallets open.

Step 2

Greet them and build rapport. It's important to sound like a breath of fresh air. Work yourself into a persona—one of friendliness and happiness. Say, "Hi [their first name]. How are you today?" Take your time with this part of the call—and be genuinely interested in the answer. If you treat the caller like a person and not just a name on a page, you're likely to get a warmer response.

Step 3

Ask for permission. This is critical, as it gives you "talking space" and the permission to discuss whatever it is you have to discuss. Say, "Would it be OK if

I outlined the reason for my call?" Alternately, try, "Can I tell you why I'm calling today?" or "Is it all right if I just cut right to the chase and tell you why I've phoned you today?"

Step 4

Outline the call. Explain precisely what you're going to say. For example, "First, I'm calling to talk to you about [problem] and a simple solution that [benefit]. Second, I wanted to talk to you about a special offer that you can take advantage of for the next 10 days—you'll save around [$]. Third, given that you like what you hear, we'll discuss how we can get started."

Make sure that you go through these points slowly. *Don't* just read them off as fast as you can. Ensure that the people on the other end are listening and understand what you have to say.

Then say, "Would it be OK if I went through the call that way?" They should say "yes." If they say it's not, say, "Could I just ask why?" If they say, "I'm too busy," you say, "That's fine, I understand. I do have something good to share with you, so I'll make a note to phone you back. I could do that later this afternoon, or tomorrow morning. Which of those is better for you?" If they say neither is, you say, "OK, give me a day and a time this week, and I'll work around that."

Step 5

Confirm that they have an interest. Qualify them by saying, "Can I just ask—do you have a problem with. . .?" A good example is, "Are you paying more tax than you want to right now?" Make your first few questions so broad and obvious that you have to get a positive response.

Step 6

Outline the key points to your solution. Say, "I've found so many people give me the same response. That's why we started our company—we help people just like you [solve the problem]."

Then, lead into some specific questions about them. Start with, "Can I just ask, what benefit do you see in [your key benefit]?" Then continue with a list of open-ended questions beginning with *what, how, when,* etc. Don't ask questions that may be answered with a "yes" or "no."

Some examples of questions are:

"What have been your experiences with buying [your type of product]?"

"How would you rate your happiness with the businesses you've dealt with in the past?"

"When were you thinking about upgrading next?"

"How often do you need [your type of product]?"

"Have you had trouble with [key frustration]?"

"Do you see a benefit in getting around that?"

Next, you need to ask a key question. A good example is: "OK, so what's most important to you when buying [your type of product or service]?" Then say, "Can you elaborate on that for me?" When you have an excellent outline of their current situation and needs, move on to the next step.

Step 7

Refer back to the offer. Say, "That's great, because we can really help you with that. You'll remember that I mentioned we have a special offer right now. [Outline offer]. That means you'll get great service and a great deal to boot. How does that fit with what you have in mind?"

If the answer is, "Sounds good," or something similar, move onto the next step. If not, say, "OK. Which parts are you unsure about?" Or, "OK. What do we need to change to make it fit with what you had in mind?"

Then say, "OK. Supposing I can give you [anything else they want], how does that fit with what you had in mind?" If they say, "Fine," then say, "Great, because I can give you [explain an alternative solution that suits better]."

Step 8

Book an appointment, or make the sale direct. It pays to assume the prospects are interested enough to want to see you, or buy right now. And considering you have proposed an ideal solution to a problem they have, there is no reason why they wouldn't want to.

Use the line, "That's great. It sounds as though we have what you're after. Assuming you're happy with what we've discussed, I could see you this afternoon at [time] or tomorrow morning at [time]. Which of those suits you best?" Or, "Assuming you're happy with that, I could get it mailed out to you today. What's your best delivery address?" Then say, "Great, and which credit card is it easiest to process it on?"

Step 9

Confirm. Say, "Excellent. It's been great to talk to you. And just for my records, is this the best number to get you on, or is there another line that suits you better?"

Last, end on a high note. "Thanks so much for your time, and I look forward to seeing you at [appointment time]. Bye for now." Or, "Great. I'm just putting that in the mail for you now. I'll phone soon to check how it's going. Bye for now."

How to Write a Door-to-Door Script

Step 1

Ensure that you are smiling before you knock on the door. A good technique is to picture the people behind the door looking happy to see you.

Step 2

Greet them and build rapport. It's important to sound like a breath of fresh air. Work yourself into a persona—one of friendliness and happiness. Say, "Hi [their first name]. How are today?" Take your time with this part of the visit—and be genuinely interested in the answer. If you treat them like people and not just another house, you're likely to get a warmer response.

Step 3

Ask for permission. This is critical as it gives you "talking space" and the permission to discuss whatever you have to discuss. Say, "Would it be OK if I outlined the reason for my visit?" Alternately, try, "Can I tell you why I'm calling today?" or, "Is it alright if I just cut right to the chase and tell you why I've come to see you today?"

Step 4

Outline the visit. Explain precisely what you're going to say. For example, "First, I'm here to talk to you about [problem] and a simple solution that [benefit]. Second, I wanted to talk to you about a special offer you can take advantage of for the next 10 days—you'll save around [$]. Third, given that you like what you hear, we'll discuss how we can get started."

Make sure you go through these points slowly. *Don't* recite them off as fast as you can. Ensure that the person is listening and understands what you have to say. Remember, you're talking *to* them, not *at* them.

Then say, "Would it be OK if I went through the visit that way?" They should say "yes." If they don't, say, "Could I just ask why?" If they say, "I'm too busy," you say, "That's fine. I understand. I do have something good to share with you, so I'll make a note to come back. I could do that later this afternoon, or tomorrow morning. Which of those is better for you?" If they say "neither," you say, "OK, give me a day and a time this week, and I'll work around that."

Step 5

Confirm that they have an interest. Qualify them by saying, "Can I just ask—do you have a problem with. . .? A good example is, "Are you paying more on your mortgage than you want to right now?" Make your first few questions so broad and obvious that you have to get a positive response.

Step 6

Outline the key points to your solution. Say, "I've found that so many people give me the same response. That's why we started our company—we help people just like you [solve the problem]."

Then, lead into some specific questions about them. Start with, "Can I just ask, what benefit do you see in [your key benefit]?" Then continue with a list of open-ended questions, beginning with *what, how, when,* etc. Don't ask questions that may be answered with a "yes" or "no."

Some examples of questions include:

"What have been your experiences with buying [your type of product]?"

"How would you rate your happiness with the businesses you've dealt with in the past?"

"When were you thinking about upgrading next?"

"How often do you need [your type of product]?"

"Have you had trouble with [key frustration]?"

"Do you see a benefit in getting around that?"

Next, you need to ask a key question. A good example is, "OK, so what's most important to you when buying [your type of product or service]?"

Then say, "Can you elaborate on that for me?" When you have an excellent outline of their current situation and needs, move on to the next step.

Step 7

Refer back to the offer. Say, "That's great, because we can really help you with that. You'll remember I mentioned that we have a special offer right now [Outline the offer]. That means you'll get great service and a great deal to boot. How does that fit with what you have in mind?"

If the answer is, "Sounds good," or something similar, move on to the next step. If not, say, "OK. Which parts are you unsure about?" Or, "OK. What do we need to change to make it fit with what you had in mind?"

Then say, "OK. Supposing I can give you [anything else they want], how does that fit with what you had in mind?" If they say fine, then say, "Great, because I can give you [explain an alternative solution that suits better]."

Step 8

Book an appointment, or make the sale direct. It pays to assume the prospects are interested enough to want to see you, or buy right now. And considering you have proposed an ideal solution to a problem they have, there is no reason why they wouldn't want to.

Use the line, "That's great. It sounds as though we have what you're after. Assuming you're happy with what we've discussed, I could see you this afternoon at [time] or tomorrow morning at [time]. Which of those suits you best?" Or,

"Assuming you're happy with that, I could get that mailed out to you today. What's your best delivery address?" Then say, "Great, and which credit card is it easiest to process that on?"

Step 9

Confirm. Say, "Excellent, it's been great talking to you. And just for my records, is this the best number to get you on, or is there another line that suits you better?"

Last, end on a high note. "Thanks so much for your time, and I look forward to seeing you at [appointment time]. Bye for now." Or, "Great, I'll go back to the office and organize that for you now. I'll phone soon to check how it's going. Bye for now."

Break-Even Analysis

As with any marketing strategy, it's essential that you work out your costs up front when devising and implementing a strategy involving scripts. Otherwise you'll have no idea what you need to achieve in order for the campaign to be worthwhile.

You may find out after doing the analysis that the campaign has little chance of success. You may discover that you need to go back to the drawing board altogether.

When talking about a Break-Even Analysis, I'm talking about an analysis for the whole campaign. After you've worked out your total fixed costs (for the campaign), you then work out your profit (your average dollar sale minus your variable costs). You should now have enough information to work out how many responses you need in order to break even.

Divide this number by the total number of prospects you are planning to approach. This will give you a percentage response rate. As a very rough guide (every case is different), anything over 15 percent is stretching it. If you need that high a response, you might need to reconsider it.

Experience shows that the very best scripts get around a 15 percent response for cold lists and 60 percent for existing customers or very warm lists. These are rare results. If you need higher than that to break even, reassess whether this is the best marketing method for you.

Work through the Analysis sheet that follows. Just fill in the answers. It couldn't be simpler than that.

Scripts
Hard Costs
Phone Calls	$ . . . .
Follow-up Material	$ . . . .
Other	$ . . . .
1. Total Fixed Costs	$ . . . .

2. Average $$$ Sale $ . . . .

Variable Costs
Telephone	$ . . . .
Wages	$ . . . .
Electricity	$ . . . .
Rent	$ . . . .
Brochures	$ . . . .
Postage	$ . . . .
Other	$ . . . .
3. Total Variables	$ . . . .

Delivery Costs
Cost of Goods Sold	$ . . . .
Taxes	$ . . . .
Transportation	$ . . . .
Packaging	$ . . . .
Other	$ . . . .
4. Total Delivery	$ . . . .

5. Net Profit [2/(3+4)] $ . . . .

$$\boxed{\textbf{Part 4}}$$

■ Customer Service

What Is Customer Service?

"Charlie, this has got to be one of the most asked, and misunderstood, questions. And it must be one of the most misunderstood concepts in business today as well. In fact, I doubt if these two words are ever used in the same sentence by many business owners, judging by the way they operate."

"I pride myself on my customer service, Brad, but I'm sure you're going to surprise me yet again by telling me things I never dreamed of."

I wasn't going to disappoint him, even though this was one area that he had made a name for himself in.

"Tighten up on this, and you're bound to make more sales than you were previously."

"So what then is customer service, Brad? How would you define it?"

"I'm glad you asked, Charlie. Customer service is nothing more than the process by which you create Raving Fans for your business. It's as simple as that."

"A what? What's a Raving Fan?"

"We'll get to that in a moment. But first, let me mention that there's a lot that goes into providing great customer service. To understand it more clearly, you need to first focus on your customers. That's right—it's all about the customers: their wants, needs, and requirements."

Who Is "The Customer"?

So who then is your customer?

If you really begin to think about it, there are four classes, or types, of customers and they're all equally important to you. Who are they? They include:

The Owners: Business must serve them by providing an acceptable level of profit.

The Team Members: Business must serve them by providing recognition, rewards, and a pay check.

The Suppliers: Business must serve them by paying their bills.

The Customers: Business must serve them by filling their needs.

As you can see, customers are a diverse group of people that come from all walks of life. They also have various and differing relationships with the business. They do have one thing in common, however. They all have needs and wants.

The needs and wants of the owners will be different than those of the team, and suppliers will certainly have different needs and wants than those who buy from the business. But they all have needs and wants. It's the job of the business to discover what those are, and then to sell them what they need.

Of course, they will be selling rather differently to owners of the business as they would to suppliers. Selling takes place on different levels. The team members have to be "sold" on the business, otherwise they'd leave and look for better employment if they didn't believe the business had a future. Owners could sell their shares if they weren't "sold" on the business's outlook by the management team. And suppliers wouldn't offer generous credit terms or prices if the business weren't "sold" to them correctly at the outset.

You need to understand that the concept of providing great customer service is all about relationship building—and this means communication.

It's a two-way street that involves an Emotional Bank Account in which you make deposits and withdrawls. You need to establish your Emotional Bank Account with your customers by first making a deposit, much as you would with an ordinary bank account. You would, for instance, make a deposit of trust, goodwill, price incentives, or the offer of a good job. Then, after you have built up a positive account through showing your customers you are genuinely interested in their needs and wants, you can begin making withdrawls. You can, only then, begin expecting your customers to start assisting you to achieve your own goals, be they reaching your sales targets, referring friends, or becoming Raving Fans.

Who Is Your Ideal Customer?

It's often said there are customers, and there are *customers*. How true this is.

There are those customers you'd love to deal with every day, and there are those you'd wish never came back. But there are more than just two basic groups. There are, in fact, four categories, A, B, C, and D. I explain them as follows:

- *Awesome*
- *Basic*
- *Can't deal with*
- *Dead*

You might wish to only deal with the A's and B's. If that's the case, get rid of the rest. How do you do that? Simple. Tell them. Or set up rules for doing business, then write to everyone on your database, explaining you're repositioning your business and here are the new rules. You can also change your pricing policy or the décor of your premises—this alone will filter out those you don't want. A video store wanted to shake off the young hooligans who had taken to gathering there. All they did was change the type of music they played in the store. Instead of playing music that teenagers listen to, they began playing classical music. Their client base changed virtually overnight.

If you were to really analyze your business, you'll find that 20 percent of your customers account for 80 percent of your business. This is what I call the 80-20 Rule. Do you know who your 20 percent is? These are the one's you should be concentrating your efforts on.

Satisfaction

Now that we've looked at the first word in "customer service," let's look at what lies behind the second. Begin by asking yourself this. Do customers leave your business feeling satisfied or delighted?

I know this is a profound question, but you do need to give it some thought. Be honest with yourself. How do your customers really feel about doing business with you?

The first thing you need to understand is that customers *expect* to be satisfied when making contact with any business. They have a need that they want satisfied. They've also gone to the trouble of finding out which businesses can satisfy that need, then they've done something about it. They've either called up or actually traveled to your business. What happens next will determine the lasting impression they have of your business.

They *expect* satisfaction, but will actually talk to others about your business if they get more than they *expect*.

So give them something to talk about.

This is the first step to creating a Raving Fan.

Good customer service is proactive. Don't wait until you have a problem in this area before doing something about it—before you think about ways and means of taking care of your customers. How can you give your customers something more than they expect?

Think of different things you could do to get them talking. Brainstorm. Consult your salespeople. Start becoming innovative in this area. Think outside the box.

Make this part of your routine. Get used to constantly searching for new ways of satisfying your customers. Keep your eyes open, watch what other businesses are doing, and keep innovating. You see, customers actually *expect* you to keep getting better.

Moments of Truth

Do you know what your Moments of Truth are? They are the times when it really counts to impress someone with your service.

Do you now know what yours might be? Take the time now to list as many of them as you can. Be ruthless with yourself. A good place to start is with your customer interaction.

Once you've jotted down some of your Moments of Truth, you'll begin to see why customers leave you for a competitor. You'll begin to develop ideas to stop this in its tracks.

Before we go any further, here's some statistics about why customers leave that may startle you. They are:

- 1 percent due to death.
- 3 percent due to a house move.
- 5 percent due to buying from a friend.
- 9 percent due to being sold by a competitor.
- 14 percent due to finding a better product or price.
- 68 percent due to perceived indifference.

These figures are staggering. Sixty-eight percent of your customers leave because they perceive your business to be indifferent to their needs. They feel that you just don't care.

Now look at how many leave because of the efforts of your opposition. The figures are so small as to be almost negligible. Only 9 percent are swayed by the active efforts of your competitors, while a mere 14 percent find a more attractive deal elsewhere.

Remember my 80-20 Rule? If you were to do really well with only 20 percent of your customers, you'd be looking after those that account for 80 percent of your revenue. So how hard is it to hang on to that 68 percent slice of customers who leave just because they think you don't care about them? Putting this another way, how easy would it be to retain that 20 percent of customers who contribute the most to your bottom line just by treating them properly? Why do all the difficult (and costly) things to shore up your bottom line when a simple remedy like offering great customer service can do it for you?

Winning Customer Service

OK. So you've decided that the level of service your business provides its customers could be a whole lot better. What do you do about it to make it the talk of the town?

Let me now share with you the three steps you must take to achieve great, and meaningful, customer service.

Step # 1. You must aim for *consistency*. It's no good if whatever you do differs each day. Your customers will want to know that whenever they visit your business, the service will be the same. And it doesn't matter what the level of customer service is, so long as it's consistent. I mean if you are running a five-star hotel you will serve your dinner guests at their tables, whereas if you were running a fast food outlet you wouldn't. This doesn't mean that the customer service at the fast food joint is inferior to that at the hotel. It would just be different, at a different level. And you must offer consistency in both service and delivery.

Step #2. Make it *easy* for customers *to buy.* You see, with consistency comes *trust.* By building consistency into your sales process, you will ensure that you systematically surpass their expectations every time they buy from you. They will begin to trust your business; they will know that every time they buy from you there will be no unpleasant surprises. They receive the same pleasant greeting each and every time they arrive, they receive the same efficient and courteous service while they are there, and their questions are answered accurately and honestly. Do everything possible to make their buying experience easy. This way, they will know what to expect when they return next time.

Step #3. Now introduce the *wow* factor. This is the way to create Raving Fans. Understand this: The fundamentals of creating great customer service involve creating a system to make sure your customers' expectations are surpassed, every time. Having satisfied customers implies you have given them all they've wanted, but nothing more. But if you're going to surpass their expectations, you must systematically go beyond their expectations. Every single day you need to be getting better. The Japanese have a good term for this. They call it "Kaizen"— constant and never-ending improvement.

To do this, you need to go further than just providing great customer service. You need to implement a customer service plan, which comprises the following action points:

- Identify your ideal customers. Find out who they are.

- Create your customer service vision. Remember, customer service is about understanding that the little things are important. You need to make an impression on your customers.

- Conduct market research. You need to ask your ideal customers what they would regard as excellent customer service.

- Now create your customers' customer service vision.

- Take the two visions and combine them to create an ultimate customer service vision.

- Decide what it is you can promise your customers. This must be something you can deliver each and every time. My rule is to underpromise and overdeliver.

- Make sure you get your team members involved. Give them the vision, and ask them for ideas on how it can be delivered. Work consistently with them on this.

- Make sure you have continual checkups. Make sure you are delivering what you promise.

- As your level of service gets better, move the goalposts. Keep improving.

- Always give your customers more than they expect. I send out gifts continually.

- And always smile. You see, people love to feel special.

People are willing to *pay* for service—when it's the service they desire. If the service exceeds their expectations, they will *stay* with you and they will *say* good things about your business.

But if your service is poor, they'll *walk* away, they'll *talk* negatively about your business, and they'll *balk* at coming back.

Be consistent, always smile, and give your customers more than they expect. That way you can be sure that they'll leave with a smile on their face.

The Ladder of Loyalty

Most good businesses spend time and money in the pursuit of good customer service so they can get customers to come back and make further purchases. But understand that good customer service in itself doesn't build customer loyalty. Take, as an example, two businesses. One gives average customer service and the other prides itself on its good customer service. If the first business writes a follow-up letter to its customers inviting them to shop there again but the second one doesn't, where do you think the customers are more likely to shop next? At the first business, even though its customer service is rated as being only average.

OK, so let's take a closer look at this very important concept—customer loyalty.

How do you build loyal customers? I like to explain this using the Loyalty Ladder concept. What I mean by this is that you have to move your customers up this ladder, and you need to keep them moving up the ladder all the time.

Think of it just like an ordinary ladder. If you were to step up onto the first rung of the ladder, would you just hang around there for a while before doing something? No, you would want to climb up right away, or get off.

Now, ask yourself why it is you want to build a Loyalty Ladder for your business. I'd suggest that it is because the first sale you make to a customer is made at a loss. Yes, statistics show 9 out of 10 first sales are made at a loss, because there are advertising costs, marketing costs, and commissions that first need to be taken into account. If you don't get that customer to come back and buy again, that customer isn't profitable to you.

Let's now take a closer look at the Loyalty Ladder and what the various stages on it involve:

1. **SUSPECT**. When they first start out on the Loyalty Ladder, right at the bottom rung, people are called suspects. How do you identify them? They are only potential customers at this stage, they fit within your target market, and they are willing to buy from you if they are in your geographic area.

2. **PROSPECT**. We then move up the ladder to prospect. Prospects are suspects who have taken some sort of action like phoning in from an ad or visiting your business. You must collect all their details so you can stay in touch. This is most important, as building customer loyalty is all about relationship building. You will be aiming to build a database of prospects. You now use all your sales skills to move your prospect one rung up the ladder to the next stage, to that of customer.

3. **CUSTOMER**. To be classified as a customer, your prospect needs to have spent money, and you need to have recorded the sale in your records. This last step may seem strange, but it is most important, because it allows you to differentiate between prospects and customers on your database. You see, if you are planning to send a letter out to all prospects offering them an incentive to buy, you don't want to be sending it to people who are already customers. This record will also tell you when they last bought, how often they buy, and what their average dollar sale is. Here's something you'll find interesting: I find most businesses put up a huge *stop* sign at this level. The salespeople seem to sit back waiting for these customers to return, instead of taking proactive steps and inviting them back. Understand that at the customer level they have cost you money. If you are content to stop at this level, your business will eventually go broke. I have eaten out at many restaurants, and guess what? I'm not on any database. I've never received a letter from any of them saying: "Brad, we'd love to have you back." This is, to my mind, quite insane. They seem to be saying; "You've bought; now I'm going to just hope like heck you come back." Think about the possibilities for your business. The *stop* sign is the scariest thing I've come across in business. You need to get rid of it, and fast.

4. **MEMBER**. When your customers make their second purchase, they become members. They now have a feeling of belonging. Understand customers who make two purchases are 10 times more likely to make more than someone who has made only one. So, you need to put some effort

into your members. Give them a membership card and a membership pack. How many of your customers know all your products? Very few, I would suggest. So why not include a product catalog in the membership pack? You can also include samples, vouchers, and things like that. One interesting example I came across recently was at a truck stop in New Zealand. The owner pinned up photographs on a notice board of all drivers who had stopped the night there. Then there's the coffee shop that gives you your own personalized coffee mug. Each time you come in, they get your mug down from the shelf for you. These two examples give members a sense of belonging.

5. **ADVOCATE.** Once you have members, you move them up the ladder to the next level—to that of advocate. An advocate is someone who sells you to other people. The criteria for advocates are that they will give referrals or promote you, and they keep buying. Advocates are one of your major capital assets.

6. **RAVING FAN.** Once you have created advocates, you need to move them up to the top of the ladder where they become Raving Fans. Understand the difference: An advocate is someone who will sell for you whereas a raving fan is someone who can't stop selling for you. The exciting thing about Raving Fans is that they can almost be regarded as part of your team. They want to see you succeed. Of course, they continue buying from you all along.

Remember, the aim of the game is to move people up from customer to Raving Fan. This is where you begin to make profit. And remember, people are prepared to *pay* for service.

Part 5

▮ Phone Power

"It's now time to think a little more proactively, Charlie. Ever wondered about how you could use your telephone as a powerful sales tool?"

"You mean by telemarketing?"

"Exactly."

I could see he was lukewarm. No spontaneous reaction this time.

"Not my style, I'm afraid," he answered, making it fairly obvious he didn't want to go there.

"You could be missing out on a wonderful opportunity, Charlie. And it doesn't necessarily involve tying you up for hours on end phoning people up at night, either. Let me explain."

What Is Telemarketing?

"Telemarketing is a form of direct marketing that generally involves communicating with prospects without the aid of an intermediary via the telephone. It typically consists of incoming and outgoing calls. Telemarketing is one of the most flexible marketing strategies available today, allowing you to adjust, fine-tune, or alter your approach as you go. You can switch target markets, change scripts, or alter your offer with just one phone call."

"No kidding!"

I had his attention once more, and his interest.

"Telemarketing is used to achieve the following:

Incoming

    Answering service.

    Message service.

Order taking.

Voice mail.

Outgoing

Appointment setting.

Lead generation.

Cold calling.

Voice mail.

Updating databases.

Sales.

Surveys.

"That gives it a slightly different perspective, doesn't it Charlie?"

"What can I say, other than keep talking?"

The Big Picture

Marketers have, in recent times, largely abused their position in the marketplace by ignoring their prospect's privacy. This has resulted in telemarketing's gaining a fairly negative image, and prospects offering strong resistance to all but the most professional of calls.

Telemarketing has become "hard work" to most marketers, but it still offers extremely good outcomes for those who know what they're doing.

Because of the constraints of the medium, impressions play a large part in telemarketing. First impressions are very important. Your first few words will create an impression in the mind of your prospect that will set the tone for the rest of the conversation. Make sure yours is a great one.

Similarly, the last impression you leave your prospect with will have a bearing on the ultimate goal of your telemarketing campaign—to covert prospects into customers.

Obviously this doesn't come easy. It takes time and practice. It also takes another important ingredient—testing and measuring. You need to be aware of whether what you're doing is having the desired effect. You need to know whether your script is working for you or getting in the way of sales. And the only way to really find this out is to test and measure.

Beliefs

Prospects only have what you tell them to gauge whether you're genuine or not. They can only go by your voice and the words you choose. So how then can you ensure that your first impression is a good one? How can you ensure that you're giving yourself the best chance possible to be heard out?

It all comes down to your beliefs. You see, if you hold strong beliefs about something, this will color what you're saying and how you say it. Firm beliefs give you conviction, confidence, and enthusiasm, and this is picked up over the phone.

What then is a belief?

A belief is something you hold to be true.

So, before you begin writing your telemarketing script, think about what your beliefs concerning salespeople, customers, and the product or service that you provide are. Then think about what you believe your target market's beliefs about these are. Understanding this will help you understand your target market better. Remember, this is essential from a marketing point of view. Think about what they normally base their purchasing decisions on. Most follow the 80-20 Rule: 80 percent emotion and 20 percent logic. Does this apply to your product or service?

What are your beliefs about money? For that matter, what is money? Think of it as nothing more than an idea backed by confidence. That's all it really is.

Communication

The essence of telemarketing is communication. The better your team members are at communicating, the better they'll be at telemarketing. You see, true communication *is* the response you get. Get it?

When you really think about it, we have only three communication tools at our disposal—the words we use, our voice, and our body language. Now here's the interesting thing: words account for only 7 percent of our communication efforts, our voice accounts for 38 percent, and body language a staggering 55 percent.

How does that leave you as a telemarketer?

Well, you may be surprised because you do have more than just words and your voice in your linguistic armory! And it falls under the "body language" category. That's right, it's called NLP, or Neurolinguistic Programming. NLP is all about communication modalities (verbs expressing a grammatical mood) and understanding how people think, make decisions, learn, and understand. There are so many NLP skills that you can use to build rapport with people. For example, by "matching and mirroring," you will be able to start building instant rapport. You will seem more trustworthy and familiar. These skills alone can win you the sale. Match their words and the tonality, pitch, pace, and volume of their speech. Then go and read as much as you can on the subject.

Furthermore, there is a Linguistic Systems Diagnostic Instrument available that helps you learn more about how you and others communicate. It's often referred to as VAK (short for Visual, Auditory, and Kinesthetic). Forty percent of people can be classified as visual, 20 percent as auditory, and 40 percent as kinesthetic. Which are you? Understanding the modalities through which your team communicates has profound implications not only for your bottom line, but also for team harmony, effectiveness, and the type of strategies that'll work best for your business. The Language System Diagnostic Instrument is a five-minute, timed test. After completing the instrument, the participants should be told their responses to the items on the instrument reflect whether they tend to respond to the world around them in a primarily visual mode, in a primarily auditory mode, or in a primarily kinesthetic (physical feeling) mode.

The DISC Behaviour Profile is another informative and useful tool that is helpful in understanding your behavior and that of others. It indicates whether you are predominantly outgoing, people oriented, reserved, or task oriented.

To find out more about these various tools, contact your *Action* Coach.

Standards

Consistency is the key to successful telemarketing. For this reason, it's imperative you operate to a set of standards. You need a system.

Here's what you do.

Performance Standard No. 1

Smile. And keep smiling until you *feel* it, but *before* you pick up the phone. Get into the right frame of mind. Imagine your prospects already have their wallets open.

Performance Standard No. 2

Answer every call after the second ring, but before the third.

Performance Standard No. 3

Greet the caller by saying, "Good Morning/Afternoon (Company Name). This is (your first name and surname). Or if your phone is being answered by a receptionist or secretary, "Good Morning/Afternoon (Company Name/Location). This is (first name) speaking. Some hints here: Never attempt to screen callers at this stage. If you need to transfer them to the appropriate team member or if you need to check something out, ask their permission to put them on hold. And never say the person they're asking for is in a meeting. Rather say he is with someone.

Performance Standard No. 4

Listen attentively and give out positive strokes.

Performance Standard No. 5

Ask questions. Always ask the magic question, "Thanks for your call. Just so I can help you best, would it be OK if I asked you a couple of questions?" This is most important because the questioning process will ultimately lead to a sale. It will help you build rapport with your caller, assist you with the selling process, and provide a reason for follow-up afterwards. Make use of a concept that I call the Question Funnel. Start with open-ended questions like *who, what, where, when, why*, and *how*. Then get more specific. Next, offer solutions based on what you have learned. Then test the caller's temperature before getting into detail. Remember to play dumb and dig deep throughout the questioning process. But more on this shortly.

You might need to use question softeners at this point to keep the process rolling. These are questions that start as follows:

- "Can I just ask. . ."
- "By the way. . ."
- "Incidentally. . ."

What you're doing here is maintaining the question cycle whereby you ask a question, listen attentively, and then provide some positive strokes.

Performance Standard No. 6

Give little pieces of information, and speak the callers' language. Always bear in mind they will be asking, "What's in it for me?" And so should you.

Performance Standard No. 7

Check the caller's temperature and ask a detailed question. You do this by asking, "How does that fit with what you had in mind?" Then assume the sale.

Performance Standard No. 8

Confirm the order and confirm their phone number. The trick to getting information here is to ask, then remain silent.

Performance Standard No. 9

Thank your caller.

Performance Standard No. 10

Make sure you hang up last, and leave your caller on a high.

Outgoing Calls

The main focus of telemarketing is, of course, outbound in nature. It's where you or a member of your team initiates a phone call to someone on your target list or database. It's also the area that proves problematical for most marketers. You see, incoming calls originate with the prospects who already have an interest in your business. They might be responding to an ad or simply calling up to find out the price of a particular item you stock. Your job then is half done. All you need to do is assist the caller towards making a decision.

However, with outgoing calls, it's a whole new ball game. The initiative is with you this time. You are "taking your chances" by calling people who aren't expecting your call. They certainly aren't thinking about the product or service you're selling, and they probably don't have an immediate need for it. Furthermore, you're probably calling them at home and interrupting their private time. The reality is that they probably view this as an invasion of their privacy.

So, how do you deal with this?

You've got to achieve four key things with your phone call. And you don't have much time to do it in. You've got to:

- Attract their *attention*.
- Spark their *interest*.
- Stimulate a *desire*.
- Move them to *action*.

The first thing you need to do to achieve this is to "get through" to your prospect. You need to "survive" the first few seconds of the call. The best way of ensuring this is, after you've introduced yourself in the appropriate manner, to ask a headline question. Then ask permission to continue. This will greatly help you to establish a level of familiarity with your prospects. Try through your questions to let the prospects realize that they need your help. Offer to mail them something, such as a catalog or brochure, then follow up with another phone call. You could also offer to fax more information to them, if this is more appropriate. What you'll be doing through this process is developing rapport. But you need to be persistent, as it could take you many phone calls (to the same people) before they'll do business with you.

You see, what you'll be doing is progressing through a script to ensure that you begin by getting their permission to outline what it is you want to say. Then you'll set in motion a process of questioning to ascertain how you can help them. This leads to solutions that you'll offer. At this point you again need to seek their agreement that the solutions are in fact solutions to a problem or a need they have. If so, the prospect can arrive at a decision. It's at this point that you now outline the investment that they need to make. This leads them to taking *Action*. Finally, seek their permission again, this time to follow up with them later on, to set an appointment, to charge their credit card, or to mail out the product. Refer back to the section on scripts for more detail on this.

It's unlikely your call will be smooth sailing from beginning to end. It's almost certain you'll have to deal with objections along the way. Unless you handle them professionally, they're likely to result in the termination of the call.

So how do you handle objections?

Here are a few basic guidelines:

- Seek *agreement* as many times as you can.
- Ask questions such as, "Are there any other reasons besides. . . ?"
- Ask, "If (the reason is taken care of), would it be OK to go ahead?"
- If they answer "no," there must be another reason preventing them from going ahead. Ask this: "Can I ask why?"
- If they answer "yes," then say, "Let's invest some time looking at (reason)."

Part 6

▪ Point of Sale

"Charlie, what we're now going to look at is a Point of Sale strategy designed to generate more sales for your business, but perhaps more importantly, I'll leave you with a selection of effective systems to get you started."

"I'm sure that what you're going to show me will be fascinating stuff, Brad, but are you sure it's applicable to the type of business I run?"

I could understand his confusion.

"Absolutely, Charlie. See, get this right and it could open up a whole new revenue stream you haven't enjoyed until now. Look at it this way. You've probably been missing out on a lucrative source of income. There are untapped dollars out there."

"Ah, I'm with you. Do you think I should be stocking aftermarket products like steering wheel covers, seat covers, cleaning products, and car care products?"

"I think you should at least give it serious consideration, Charlie. You see, unless you do, you'll never know. So let's get started, shall we?"

What Is a Successful Point of Sale System?

Basically, any Point of Sale System that results in increased sales can be considered successful. The objective of your Point of Sale System is not to amuse your clients as they stand in line at your checkouts. It's to get them buying products they may not have otherwise considered.

As you probably know, to get new customers, you need to invest money in marketing. This means you have an acquisition cost for all new customers you get. Your acquisition cost is determined by how much your marketing costs are, divided by how many customers it brings into your store. Once you've calculated this figure, you can then work out how many times customers need to purchase from you before they become profitable. In the average business, this will mean selling to them two times before you begin to make a profit.

Your Point of Sale System is the tool you use to not only convert your prospect to a customer, but also to increase your number of transactions and your average dollar sale. If your customers buy the bare minimum from you, you'll actually be losing money each time you acquire a new customer. By using a well-thought-out Point of Sale System, you increase the amount of money customers spend with you, thus turning them into profitable customers.

What Makes a Successful Point of Sale System?

There are a number of key elements which, when combined, go to making up a successful Point of Sale System. The most important of these is the selling message. You'll find out which types of messages work best later.

Another important consideration is any offers you're making. No matter how well written or entertaining your Point of Sale System is, if you don't make great offers, it will not bring you additional sales.

In the following pages, you'll learn how to write point of sale headlines that work, how to position your poster for maximum impact, and which typefaces have the best recognition rates. You'll discover how to use sales scripts, how to position slow-moving stock, and which angles and appeals work best.

Testing and Measuring

Before you get started, it's critical you understand the principal of testing and measuring.

Just the same way you'd try different ads in the paper to see which one works the best, you need to be prepared to change your counter displays around and find out which approach works the best.

Remember, it's always better to hand out 20 newsletters, catalogs, or brochures that don't work, than 20,000. Even if you love your new system, and everyone who sees it goes crazy, it's important to keep your head, and avoid going too far too soon.

Take it slow at first, check the response, and then gradually increase the numbers. If you hand out 100 marketing pieces, and find that 10 of the coupons or ads come back, it should follow that 10,000 pieces should turn into 1000 additional sales.

Of course, nothing is ever that certain in marketing or business, and you really have to wait and see. Having said that, it's important to realize that if you hand out 100 pieces and see none back, you'd be a little insane to expect 10,000 to do much better.

You have the option of creating a number of versions of your Point of Sale material, and trying all versions at the same time. Ask people what they think of the material you're testing. Over time, you may notice that one version seems to do much better than the other. This is the one you keep.

The problem is, creating Point of Sale material can be expensive. There are the setup costs, then the printing costs to bear in mind. If you were to create multiple versions, you'd end up spending quite a deal more than if you just decided on one and stuck to it.

Ultimately, it depends on how important these pieces are to your business. If they represent one of your most critical sources of new business and repeat sales, then it may be in your best long-term interests to pay for a variety of marketing pieces.

The other option is to create a small number (about 20) of each version you're thinking about using. Show these to as many people as you can—customers, friends, family. When they give you feedback, *listen* to what they have to say. Don't block out their criticism of your favorite design, or minimize their praise of the one you didn't like.

It pays to not be sensitive about it—this isn't fine art we're talking about. Your marketing pieces are a business tool that is designed to make you money. Take note of what people say, and act accordingly.

When creating different versions, you should only really alter the most important parts. Changing the size of your phone number from 12 points to 16 points is unlikely to make much difference, but a new headline, a different offer, and a change in the amount of text will make a big difference.

If you're going to test a few versions against each other, make sure they are significantly different. There's no point spending all that money, only to put out a number of pieces that look virtually the same, except for a couple of truly unimportant differences.

You'll find changing the headline and the subheadlines in the main content will completely change the amount of response you get.

Just as your marketing handouts are an advertisement for your business, the headlines are the ads for the text of each Point of Sale display.

Compare these two headlines:

"How to make more money. . ."

OR

"How 37,600 women under 27 are making $2,300 per week, every week, without fail."

Which one would you read? The second headline definitely stimulates a lot more curiosity. Having said that, you can never be entirely sure which one will work the best. This is why testing and measuring is so important.

If you can understand that two headlines would bring in such a different response, you can understand why it's worth printing up a few versions and seeing which one takes off for you.

It's also important that you really take proper note of which one is working the best. Create a tally sheet and make sure you fill it in every time somebody buys off one of your Point of Sale displays. After a month or so, add up the tally and see which one is working the best.

The Seven Steps to Point of Sale Success

Step 1: Who Is Your Target Market?

If you don't know who your target market is, it's almost impossible to attract it. Imagine trying to get a date without knowing which gender you're interested in. You'd have to take the "let's see" approach. Unfortunately, the "let's see" method of marketing tends to fail every time. You won't see anything, especially in the way of repeat business.

You need to know exactly who you're dealing with, what they're interested in, and what's going to make them buy your products. If you don't know, you're really just taking your chances.

So let's get specific. Who are the people most likely to be interested in your product or service? Here are some guidelines:

Age: How old are they? Don't just say "all ages" or "a variety." We want to create a picture in mind of your average customer.

Sex: Are they male or female? "Half and half" is too broad.

Income: How much do they make? Do they earn a great living, or are they scraping for every dollar, always looking for a deal. It's essential that you find this out.

Where do they live? Are they local, or do they come from miles around to deal with you?

What are their interests? If you don't know what they're interested in, how can you design a Point of Sale System that will capture their attention? If you focus only on writing headlines you find interesting, rather than the ones your customers will find interesting, your Point of Sale System will fail.

Step 2: Where Should You Place Your Material?

Ask most businesses what they hope to achieve with their Point of Sale System and you'll get the same response—more sales. Of course, this is exactly what you want to achieve, but aren't you forgetting something?

Your Point of Sale System can be an ideal tool for gathering a database. Imagine if all customers who came to your store were placed on a database. You could send them marketing material whenever you want. Of course, once you have them on your database, you can start to add their friends and family to it, making it grow in no time.

But understanding that the main focus of your campaign should be on additional sales, you need to put some thought into where your material is going to go. But first, let's have a closer look at exactly what a Point of Sale System really is.

Many people think a few posters near their registers constitutes a Point of Sale System, but it's not really that simple. Shelf talkers, catalogs, brochures, business cards, and flyers can also be classed as part of your Point of Sale System. So as you can see, some thought needs to go into the placement of these items.

To understand where to place all these different marketing pieces, you need to understand the habits of your customers. For example, when they walk through your store, do they read the posters you have on the end of each aisle, do they look at the signs you have around the store to find the right section, or do they simply walk down each aisle?

If they don't pay any attention to the posters at the ends of your aisles, then maybe you need to make them larger, or change the color or wording. You should also then ensure that your shelf talkers are placed near the various items along each aisle that you're trying to move. These need to have a strong selling message, and you need to make sure they're clearly visible.

The other thing to consider is where they look when they're standing at your counter or cash register waiting to be served. Take a moment to watch from a distance, and make a note of where the majority of them appear to be looking. It pays to do this a few times over the course of a week, so that you get a clear idea of what the average person does.

If you find that they simply stand there looking impatient, you may need to change your counter or checkout area to make it easier for them to see your Point of Sale material.

Remember, you'll need to have things at eye level if you want your customers to take notice of it. Of course, if you have long lines of people waiting from time to time, it would pay to have catalogue and brochure racks along the way that they could flip through or take with them.

A good way to make sure your racks are in the right place is to have a bar that guides them into the area where you want them to stand. Now, I know this sounds a bit like you're building a stock race for sheep, but have you ever paid attention to how people look when they're in a line? It's really not that dissimilar.

As I mentioned earlier, your Point of Sale material can be a great way to gather names for your database. Unconverted prospects should also be added to your company's mailing list. The reason for this is quite simple—the fact that they didn't buy from you the first time doesn't mean that they won't buy from you in the future. You've invested money in getting them to visit you in the first place, so why not invest a little more in getting them to come back?

There can be a variety of reasons why people don't buy from you initially. Perhaps you didn't have the exact model they were after, or maybe they weren't in a position to buy at that time. By keeping in contact with them, you give yourself the chance of doing business with them in the future. Even if they have bought from someone else, you might be able to pick up some business from them for their parts and accessories.

When you really think about it, the more people who are on your database, the more sales you'll make from it. All you need to make your business a success is a database of prospects to mail to.

Step 3: What Do You Want to Say?

There's often heated debate about which type of Point of Sale material works best, but there's never a disagreement about which type doesn't, and that's those with no obvious purpose.

For example, if you wrote a flyer or poster that says, *Hi, we sell computer disks. We've been doing it for 12 years*, it's unlikely people will feel the urge to buy. Your material needs to give them a good reason to read, then a great reason to do something about dealing with you.

Your material needs to have a clear purpose, and take people from Point A to Point B. Point A is your headline, which should identify where they are now. The body of the piece leads them to Point B, which is where you tell them why they should act right now, and how to do it.

Most important is understanding your customers. If you understand their needs, wants, and position, you can sell almost anything to them. If you nail the *appeal* and the message, you'll win.

Your Point of Sale material must do one of two things—provide a solution to a problem the prospects are having right now, or introduce them to something new that appeals. If it doesn't do one of these two things, and do it in a very specific and direct way, you need to ask yourself what the material is designed to do.

You must decide on who you want to target, what you want to say to them, and what you want them to do as a result of reading your Point of Sale material.

For instance, if you want people to buy a case of computer disks on their way out of your store, think about what you need to say to encourage them to do that.

What about, *"Don't wait until you've run out of disks. Grab a pack of 25 for only $5.95."*

This headline identifies the situation and offers the deal up front. It takes the prospect from Point A *(Don't run out of computer disks—here's an alternative)* to Point B *(The alternative is affordable and easy).*

It pays to remember that simply asking people to act now (or for that matter, telling them to act now) is rarely enough. You need to give them a good reason why *now* is the time to do something.

See, most purchases can be delayed forever. It's one thing to create desire, but it's another to actually get people to part with their cash. Every buyer has priorities. There are, of course, ways of rearranging them.

The other thing to bear in mind when writing Point of Sale material is the amount of information you should include. If you have to explain too much, perhaps you should look at another method. Remember, your customers may be in a hurry and not want to stand at your counter reading a long-winded marketing piece.

Of course, it depends on the quality of your information and the offer itself. If your headline is *"I have videotapes of what you did behind your partner's back"* and your offer is *"ask the sales person when you get served and you can have them back,"* you could fill a whole poster in small type—the prospect would read every word.

Generally though, it's best to keep it short and punchy. The general format is, *"Hey you, here's a great deal. Here's why you should take it up, and here's why you should do it now."*

If you have to say too much more than that, you should give some thought to whether Point of Sale material is the right way to go.

Step 4: How to Put Together Your Point of Sale System

Now that we've covered the basics, it's time to get into the nuts and bolts of how to construct your Point of Sale System.

First, let's look at all the elements that go into making the ultimate Point of Sale System.

Shelf Talkers

No, these are not people who stand next to your shelves telling people how good your products are. These are the signs you place on shelves that list the benefits and key features of each product.

Now, I don't mean every product in your store. Shelf talkers need to be used sparingly, or people will start to ignore them. You should place them only under any products that are new in your store, that are on sale, or those you're desperately trying to move.

Now, shelf talkers can be as simple as a sign saying, *"Was $29.95, now only $12.95!!!"* But more commonly they'll list the key benefits of the product in bullet-point form. For example:

- **Easy to Clean**
- **Won't Rust**
- **Simple to Use**

Because people will most likely just be glancing over these shelf talkers, it's important not to cram too much information onto them. A good powerful headline, and the key benefits stated clearly will do the job. If customers need any further information, they can read it on the pack or they can ask a member of your sales team.

Posters

Posters form the backbone of any Point of Sale System. They can be placed throughout the store or at your register so people seeing them as they shop are encouraged to take action. They're also a great way to draw attention to any flyers or catalogs you have on your counters.

We'll talk more about the construction of posters and flyers (which are in some ways just miniposters anyway) in general advertising later in this section, but there are a few key points you need to understand.

Your posters are a bit like a billboard. People will be walking past them quickly, so you can't place too many words on them. People generally don't have the time, or the inclination, to stand in front of a poster for any great length of time. Your poster is only there to get them interested enough to find out more. They can do this by looking at the product or asking a member of your team.

If the aim of your poster is to grab attention, it needs to be *big, bold,* and *colorful*. And if it's to be successful in making sales, it needs to have a strong selling message.

It's possible your suppliers will already have posters made up. In fact, you'll probably find most suppliers will have a complete Point of Sale System for each of their products. But understand that these companies are only promoting their own goods, and their material should only complement your system. It should not be viewed as your system.

If your suppliers don't have a system you can use, why not offer to make up posters promoting their product? You can then ask them to help cover the cost of printing. This is known as cooperative advertising or supplier subsidy. The way it works is simple. The majority of suppliers calculate an advertising fee into the prices they charge you for their goods. This is designed to cover the cost of any advertising you run to promote their products. Now your suppliers are unlikely to tell you this is the case. Obviously, if you don't ask for the money, they get to keep it. But they are usually happy to help with the cost of the advertising, provided it's within reason. Some suppliers won't give you money towards it, preferring to give you stock at cost instead. But let's face it; selling stock at a higher markup makes you more money anyway.

Promotional Cards

If you've got people standing at your counter waiting to be served, it's a great opportunity to give them a promotional card. Now let me explain what I mean by promotional cards.

Let's say you've got a loyalty or bonus club that you're just starting. Now these clubs will usually have a card attached to them. By that I mean customers who are involved in the campaign will have a VIP card or a bonus card that rakes up points for them each time they make a purchase. Alternately, they might be collecting stamps on their cards to get some prize or reward when they reach a certain total. If you have posters or pamphlets that explain how they can participate in the promotion, the chances are you'll get a lot more people joining in. This is particularly true if you tell people to ask a member of your team how to join when they get served.

Another good idea is to have scratch cards, which are given to customers when they spend a certain amount of money. The card works similar to Instant Scratch-It cards where panels are scratched off for the chance to win a prize.

Now if you have posters or flyers that explain what they can win, and how much customers have to spend to get a card, the chances are they'll buy something extra just to get a card. Obviously, people are not going to buy something they don't need, but they might purchase something they do need earlier than what they otherwise might have.

Product Bins

As you're no doubt aware, a product bin is not a garbage receptacle where you throw slow-moving stock. You definitely place slow-moving stock in them, but not for the purpose of throwing it away.

Product bins are the tables, or core flute bins, that you fill with any items you're trying to sell off cheaply. For example, a hardware store might have a number of small hand tools they're trying to get rid of. This might include things like spanners, screwdrivers, and hammers.

There may be many reasons why the store's getting rid of them: they may need to make space for new stock, they might have discovered these tools are of poor quality, or simply that they've been sitting on the shelf for months. Whatever the reason, product bins are a good way to get the stock sold.

But obviously there are a few things you need to keep in mind when considering the use of product bins. First, you need to be offering huge savings. In some cases you're better off selling the stock at cost just to get rid of it. It would be ridiculous to think that simply by placing them on a display, they'll sell at full price. If they haven't sold at that price for the past four months, what makes you think they will now?

Another thing you need to put some thought into is how to draw attention to your tables or bins. The obvious and possibly most effective way is through placement. Having your product bins placed in high-traffic areas, like the middle of your main aisle, will get things moving. Another good place is near your cash register so people can rummage through the items while they wait. There's a good chance that they'll grab a few extra items before they leave.

You should also consider having large signs on, or above, the bins that indicate what great savings are on sale. Things like "Nothing over $10" or "50 percent OFF" will get people looking. You might like to have a flashing light on the bins to attract customers' attention as they walk past. These lights are also good for roving specials, where you have a time-limited sale on various items throughout your store. You simply move the light to the next items that you're discounting (normally 20–30 percent), and then have someone announce the deals via a microphone or amplifier.

Video Catalogs

Don't ever limit yourself to stationary signage and displays when putting together your Point of Sale System. There are many other opportunities you can look at that will give your system the edge. Among those are video displays or "Video Catalogs."

The way this works is quite simple. You place a TV and video near the products you're trying to promote or near the store counter. You then run a continuous-loop promotional tape. By that, I mean the tape keeps playing over and over. On many new video machines, this can be as simple as setting repeat on the machine itself.

Video catalogues have a number of significant advantages, not the least of which is the ability to demonstrate a product being used. Imagine if you had a new mop that could soak up any type of spillage. Now you could have posters and signage that would tell the customer what it does, but imagine the benefit of actually being able to *show* them what it can do. This is one part of your system that's sure to make you more sales.

It's not uncommon to see people gathered around these promotional televisions watching goods being "put through their paces." It can generate huge amounts of interest and increased store traffic. One of the ways in which it does this is by using both sight and sound. Because the pictures are moving and not stationary, they tend to catch the consumers' eyes. But what if they're looking the other way? Well, you then get a second chance with the commentary or sounds from the TV set.

So where do you get these tapes? You basically have two worthwhile options, and no, shooting the tape yourself with a home handy cam is not one of them. You can't afford to have anything that looks tacky.

Your first option is to contact your suppliers and see what they have in the way of promotional videos. Some companies invest a great deal of money having good-quality tapes made up, and will be more than happy to supply you with a copy, free of charge. The other way is to get someone to shoot a video for you. This is particularly effective if you want to demonstrate a service that you offer.

Even if you don't take the products out of the box, but merely have someone walking around your store explaining the benefits of different items, you'll find it to be an effective tool.

Now there are any number of companies that specialize in this type of work. You can normally find them by looking in your local phone book. Their prices do vary, and you need to work out how many sales you have to make for it to be a profitable venture. If you don't believe you can make the money back, then video catalogs might not be for you.

Audio Tapes

Smart businesspeople have tapes produced that play to their customers when they phone in and are placed on hold. These same tapes can be used to play through your store's PA system so people can listen to them while they shop.

These tapes can be made up to promote any specials you're currently running, or to talk about any new products or services you offer. But it's not a good idea to have them playing all day long. Listening to the same thing over and over again will drive your team crazy. You're best to just run them for an hour or so during the store's busy times.

Checklists

This is a must. If you don't have a number of Point of Sale checklists scattered throughout your store, you've been missing out on thousands of dollars in extra revenue. Let me show you why.

Imagine you own a paint store. Now, customers who are looking to paint their house will come in and buy a few cans of paint from you. They'll probably also buy a paintbrush or roller to paint with. But how many other things are they going to need as well? You need to have a checklist for them to look over. This lists all the accessories they'll need to get the job done. For starters, they'll probably need drop cloths for any spillage or drips off the brush, a tray for the roller, a few different roller pads, a paint mixer/stirrer, maybe a ladder, thinners, overalls, something to clean the brushes in, and maybe a few different-sized brushes.

Now if you print up a checklist and have it strategically placed around your store with a sign above it that says, *"Don't even start painting your home until you've read this,"* you're certain to make additional sales.

Now while the example of the paint store is an obvious one, how many additional products could you potentially sell to your customers? For example, a motorbike store could have a checklist that includes gloves, boots, chains, oil, and cleaning products. A gardening store could list items like hoses, sprinklers, timers, and shovels. You just need to look around your store and work out what else you can on-sell.

Handy Hints-and-Tips Flyers

Often referred to as project sheets, hints-and-tips flyers are a guaranteed winner for many businesses. Picture this: A client walks into a store to buy a few things when he sees a rack containing handy tips on how to make picture frames. He starts reading, and the next minute he's hooked. You've started making sales you otherwise wouldn't have made.

Let's have a closer look at this system.

Imagine a hardware store that had project sheets on how to prepare your house for painting, or how to lay pavers in your garden. This sort of free information is sure to be a winner, even with people who aren't looking to paint their houses, or put a path in their gardens. Clients will hold onto this information so they can refer back to it at a later date.

Flyers like this have the added benefit of allowing you to showcase your expertise. By answering some of the many questions your clients have, you can show that for first-class information and advice, yours is the only store to turn to.

You receive another, more subtle, benefit by including these marketing pieces. It comes in the form of getting people to buy more products, and to embark on projects they might otherwise not have considered.

To give you an idea of how this might work, let's consider the hardware store again. Now if they were to run a spring article talking about painting the exterior of your home, explaining that this was the best time to do it, there's a good chance people might "take the bait" and decide to do it. The salesperson can then go on to list the best products to use, and include a special offer on some, or all, of those products.

Place these project sheets in their own racks around your store, and see how quickly they start paying for themselves. For the cost of a few cents to photocopy them, you won't find a more cost-effective marketing tool.

Catalogs and Brochures

Although it's an obvious choice for any Point of Sale System, very few people ever consider including their company catalogs and brochures. But it really does make sense to promote them in this fashion. I come across businesses all the time that have a group of loyal customers who don't have any idea of the range of products and services the company offers. Sure, they understand that they can get what they came in for, but they don't realize that the company offers so many other services. By leaving your brochures in a place where people can pick them up and browse through them, you have a chance to educate them on the spectrum of products and services you offer.

Simply place them on a stand with a sign that says, "Please Take One." You could, of course, use a strong selling headline. You'll find out more about writing those in a moment.

Educating your clients on everything you do is just one of the things you need to consider. When you have a sale, it's a good idea to have your catalogs spread around the store to encourage people to grab a bargain while they're there. I've seen many businesses that place their catalogs on the counter for people to pick up as they leave. But when you think about it, isn't it better to give it to them when they come in?

I mean really, they've just made the effort to drive to your store, find a parking spot, come in, and wait at your checkout, and now you want them to go home, realize they should've bought a bargain, and then come back again? It's a bit too much to ask.

A better idea is to have them on a counter or table near your front door so they can grab one on the way in. Or if you have spare team members, you could have them handing those items out to people as they come in. This would be a great way to break the ice and get the customers to tell you what they're looking for.

But no matter how you use them, you'll find that including brochures and catalogs in your Point of Sale System will add dollars to your bottom line.

Newsletters and Business Cards

Just as catalogs and brochures should be included in your Point of Sale System, so too should your newsletters. While your brochures explain your full range of products and services, and your catalogs have the benefit of letting your customers know what's on sale, having your customers browse through your newsletter has many worthwhile benefits for your business.

Your newsletter is your chance to showcase your expertise, and has the advantage of letting people know of any upcoming events. To fully understand how your newsletter can assist you in making additional sales, you need to understand the sections that should be included in any newsletter. These include the following:

Product Reviews

People who are interested in your products or services will always be interested in finding out about new products, or in the case of a service-based business, new techniques. Therefore, previewing new products will ensure a high readership. Of course, it will also generate increased sales. Customers are always looking for the latest and greatest, which makes this section of your newsletter a must.

Tips and Hints Section

The best way to ensure people not only read your newsletter but also start to collect each new issue is to include some handy hints. I've already mentioned the importance of having project sheets and handy hints flyers as part of your Point of Sale System. Having an additional section in your newsletter will double the benefits.

Upcoming Events

People like to know what's going on and hate to miss out on something special. Therefore, you should include an upcoming events section in your newsletter. There are a number of things you can include here, from upcoming sales and promotions to products that are due for release. Whatever you include, you're sure to see an increase in sales.

Introduce Your Team

One of the real benefits of newsletters is that they make your customers feel a part of what's happening in your business. They're being kept up-to-date with upcoming events and any changes to your stock or services, so they have the feeling of knowing what's going on. A good way to add to this feeling of being "part of the team" is by introducing your team members in a profile section. You see, people buy from people, not companies. By letting people know a bit more about who they're dealing with, it makes them feel more comfortable buying from them.

Sales Sections

Ads and selling messages are the most important parts of your newsletter. You need to include a strong call to action in your ads, and even at the end of each article that relates to a product or a service. If your articles get your clients interested in buying, you need a call to action to actually get them to do something. Coupons are a great way to make extra sales from your newsletters, and should be included where possible.

As you can see, there are many ways in which your newsletter helps you make additional sales. As with catalogs and brochures, you need to have them somewhere where the customers can see them and pick them up. But unlike brochures and catalogs, the idea is to have your customers pick them up as they leave so they can take the time to read them at home.

Of course, your business cards should also be given to customers at the Point of Sale. Simply setting them on the counter in a cardholder is not enough. You need to be actively handing them out. But before you do that, you must make sure your business cards are the type that will actually generate extra business.

A business card is, theoretically, a mobile advertisement for your business that works continuously. Every time customers open their wallets, you're right there, reminding them that you exist.

There are two important things to consider when designing your cards.

First, is there anything about your business card that gives the customer a reason to hang onto it? Is it anything more than just a statement of the business's name and your contact details? If customers want to contact you again, they'll hang onto it. If they're not sure, they'll probably throw it away.

Second, does it encourage the customer to call you? Does it actually *sell* for you? Perhaps you're thinking a business card can't sell. Wrong! A business card can sell like nothing else.

The important thing to remember is that a business card is nothing more than a miniflyer, a little advertisement that can fit into someone's wallet or purse. It's like giving someone one of your flyers and saying, "Here, hang onto this." A well-designed business card should be part of any Point of Sale System.

USP and Guarantee

Two things you should consider promoting through your Point of Sale material are your USP and any guarantees you have. Your USP (Unique Selling Proposition) is the one thing that is truly different about you, or at least, the one thing you can promote as being different.

A successful USP should be:

- Truly unique.
- Exciting to your target market.
- Something that will have your customers telling their friends about it.
- Something that can't be easily copied.

A lot of business owners wonder why they need a uniqueness at all—shouldn't there be room for dozens of "me-too" businesses? The fact is, there isn't, and the "me-too" businesses will ultimately go to the wall.

If you don't have an existing USP, you'll need to find one. Start by reading my book *Instant Leads*. Then write down everything you do that could be considered to be even a little bit unique. These points don't have to be earth shattering—just different enough to stand out.

To get your mind started, here is a list of some possible USP's you could adopt:

- You sell a higher quality product or service, and you can specifically show how it benefits the customer in a meaningful way.
- You provide better customer service and you can easily explain and promote why you're better.
- You offer a better or longer guarantee and you have it written down.
- You offer more choice, selection, or options, and this is something people want and always look for.
- You offer a trade-in program and no one else does.
- You serve a specific (yet sizable) demographic group that is overlooked by most competitors.
- You offer a better, more generous bonus points or loyalty club system, and your product or service is at least as good.
- You have the best after-sales service, and this is something you can explain to people easily when they buy.
- Your product or service has unique features people care about.
- You offer attractive products or services that no one else does.
- You have a "special ingredient."
- You install and deliver for free.

These are just a few examples of unique, salable points. If you think hard enough about it, you're sure to find something that you are currently doing that is unique or, more likely, something you *should* be doing that would make you unique.

Basically, your uniqueness comes from one of these seven areas: quality, price, service, delivery, speed, convenience, and experience. Regardless of what it is, you need to promote it at every available opportunity. There's no better place to start than with your Point of Sale material.

This then, is a summary of the things you need to include in your Point of Sale System. But that's only the first part of what you need to know. You also need to know how to write the copy, place any photographs, and construct top headlines. What you'll find in this next section are general advertising tips that apply to other areas of your business as well.

General Advertising

Whether you're writing a newsletter, a poster, shelf talkers, or a project sheet, these principles will apply to all. If you'd like to delve deeper into this subject, read my books *Instant Advertising* and *Instant Promotions*.

So let's now have a look at the things that make your advertising sell.

Headlines

The most important part of any advertisement, poster, flyer, or other marketing piece for that matter, is the headline. David Ogilvy, one of the all-time great direct-response copywriters, once said that 10 times as many people would read the headline as will read the rest of the marketing piece. So if you get the headline wrong, you can kiss 90 percent of your advertising dollars goodbye.

One of the things you need to keep in mind is that the headline needs to take up at least 25 percent of your advertisement or marketing piece. Before you finalize your Point of Sale headlines, write down between 10 and 20 options and ask your friends and team members which ones they like best. Then go with the most popular.

Typefaces

The typeface or font you use in your marketing pieces can make a big difference in the results you achieve. The two basic types are sans serif and serif fonts. Sans serif fonts don't have the little "feet" at the bottom of each letter. Studies have shown that people find these fonts far more difficult to read than serif fonts. Serif types have the little "feet" or "hooks" at the bottom of each letter. These "feet" appear to form a line under the words that your eye can follow. This isn't anything to worry about when choosing a font for a headline, but it certainly matters when you have a long block of text.

The most common serif font is Times New Roman. The most common sans serif font is Arial. Times give a more classic feel, while Arial seems more modern. Computers offer a huge range of fonts, and it's cheap and easy to lay your hands on some more. You may end up with too much choice, which will ultimately slow you down.

It's best to choose a basic font that looks good, and suits your image. Try and use a serif font for the main body text. Your printer or graphic designer will almost certainly recommend Arial or Helvetica (both are sans serif fonts). To their artistic eyes, Times New Roman just looks plain. Don't worry about that. The fonts you use in your headlines will give your advertising material character. The font you use for your main text just needs to be easy to read.

Point Size

The size of the font you use is referred to as point size. Studies have shown that readership does not drop off between 14 and 7-point size. As a general rule 9 or 10 points are ideal. Obviously, the larger the font, the easier it is to read, so try to keep it as large as possible.

Highlighting Text

Use bold type to highlight key points in your body copy, as well as headlines and subheadlines. Italics can also be used to highlight key areas of text, although it can be hard to read and should be used only sparingly. Never use all capitals. The only time you can is in a short headline, or for extra emphasis on single words.

To make your material easier to read, break your copy up into paragraphs. Indenting your paragraphs, rather than leaving a line between them, can cut down on wasted space. Also consider using a drop cap first letter. It's a great way to attract the eye of your customer.

Subheadlines

Subheadlines have three major benefits. They include:

- Break up large blocks of text, making it easier to read. If your copy looks like one big "chuck" of text, it can put people off. By using subheadlines you can break your copy up by giving it some "space."

- Allow someone skimming over your material to only read the points that interest them.

- Spark the readers' interest. If your headline doesn't get them in completely, you can get a second chance with your subheadlines.

It is important your subheadlines tell a story. They need to be able to convey your message to those people who are just browsing through your advertising material.

Body Copy

You get only one chance with a potential customer, so your first 50 words are crucial. You must arouse your readers' curiosity immediately, with the very first paragraph. If they're not excited after the first 50 words, they won't read the rest of your article or ad.

Use the bare minimum of copy to get your message across. Don't ramble on. But make sure you include enough information to get your readers interested enough to call you. When writing any sort of marketing piece you should never tell the whole story. Tell them as much as you need to, to get them to ask one of your team members for more information. You see, by holding back some information, you make it necessary for them to have to ask to find out more.

As far as your marketing pieces go, they should tell a story and be easy to read. When you finish writing your piece, get someone to look over it and critique it for you.

Pictures

Studies have shown flyers and posters containing a picture that takes up between 25 and 75 percent of the total advertisement have greater readership levels than those without one. You will probably need to put a fair amount of text in your material, so 25 percent is probably the ideal size.

Pictures are also an important part of any promotional material. People are generally very visual, and therefore attracted to photographs. Note: I said photographs and not line drawing or clip art. You see, line drawings and clip art look tacky. People are used to seeing photographs and are far more attracted to them.

So wherever possible, you should always use photographs in your pieces. The only exceptions should be small, humorous clip art pictures or line art in the form of technical drawings. For example, if you want to show the inner working of a new watch, you might use a line-drawing cross section to demonstrate the point you're trying to make.

Using real photographs can present a problem for some people who want to create their Point of Sale System themselves on their own computers. If you're considering this option, you'll need to consider these points:

For starters, you'll need some way to place them electronically into your marketing pieces. Scanners are one way of doing this. A reasonable flatbed scanner will cost you less than $200. But if you didn't want to go to this expense (you still need to take the photo and have it developed in the first place), you could always ask a friend to scan it and save it on disk for you. Alternately, there are companies who will scan pictures for you at a price. Many photo labs offer this service, but the feasibility of having this done will depend on how many pictures you're scanning a year, and how much each scan costs you. It may work out cheaper just to buy a scanner and be done with it.

Another way you can place photographs in your marketing pieces is by using a digital camera. Now, a digital camera will cost you around $500 to buy, but you can rent them for much less. The trick here is to rent one for a day, then take all the pictures that you think you'll use over the course of the year. Now, it obviously won't be possible to take photographs of all the new products that you'll be previewing, as many of them won't have been released when you rent the camera. But for those few exceptions, it's probably worth getting them scanned by your local photo lab.

Always put a caption under your photo. People read the captions, so make sure you take advantage of this opportunity to get them to start reading your article. While people will find your material far more interesting if you include a few photographs, just throwing a few pictures in there won't work. You need to put some thought into the types of pictures you use and their positions.

Photographs of your premises (crowded restaurants or clubs) or your products are suitable for use in newsletters, brochures, or flyers. The pictures need to back up your story. For example, a photograph of people having a great time in your club would help convince people that your establishment is a fun place to be.

You can also use photographs of people using your product or service. These can be used to educate people on what it is that you do. This can also be a great way to teach people how easy it is to use your product.

Consider putting a photo of yourself in marketing material like your newsletter. People buy from people, not companies, so let them see the people behind the company name. Place photos so they look straight out off the page or towards your body copy. If your pictures look into your article, your potential customers will also be drawn into it.

Color

It could be argued that because people see in color, your Point of Sale material should be printed in color. While this would seem a worthwhile argument, it pays to remember that most newspapers are printed in black and white. People are used to reading them, so why not your marketing material?

Printing your posters and flyers in color will cost quite a bit more than in standard black text on white paper. The aim of your marketing material is to get customers spending more with you. Obviously then, the less you need to invest to get them spending more, the better. If your headlines promise a benefit, your copy conveys your message, and your offer is worthwhile, it could be argued that you have no need for color.

But most importantly, you need to ask yourself whether your material is going to stand out well enough to be read, or will it be completely ignored? This is something you'll have to guess at to an extent, but it would pay at least in the early stages to keep the costs as low as possible.

If you're going to use any color at all, you'd be well advised to print in full process color. Research has shown that the difference between two-color and black-and-white advertising material is minimal and doesn't justify the extra expenditure.

Printing on colored paper is an inexpensive way to brighten up your material. But be careful which color paper you choose, as it can make your text difficult to read. Keep this in mind if you decide to print your text in color. As a general rule, you're far better off printing your text in black, as this will increase readability.

If you're going to use colors, it's worth noting the impact of color psychology. This is the study of how people are motivated by, or respond to, different colors. While some colors will appeal to your clients and give them a good impression of your business, others will have the opposite effect. Here are a few examples:

- Forest Green—appeals to the wealthy but may cause rejection in other economic groups

- Burgundy—same as forest green

- Bluish Red—appeals to women

- Yellowish Red—appeals to men

- Orange—makes people think the business is informal and open to everyone

- Yellow—gets attention, but can indicate cheapness

- White—good color for décor; reminds people of dairy products and cleanliness

- Red—if it relates to food, it is an appetite-enhancing color

- Blues/greens—in the food industry these are appetite suppressants

Ultimately, I recommend that you trust your own instincts before worrying about the rules. Your opinion is just as valid as anybody else's. For example, light blue will always be associated with clear skies. Red always means stop, and green generally means go, or nature.

One strong recommendation—keep it simple! Using too many colors will only make your marketing material look like a technicolor nightmare.

The fewer colors, the better. Limit yourself to about three (not including the photos, which will be full color), and then tastefully apply them to your marketing pieces.

Layouts

It's important to always consider, when designing your layout, the ease with which the publication can be read and understood. Many people fall into the trap of trying to jazz their posters and flyers up by adding different shapes and elements. Unless you have a good deal of artistic ability, you're best sticking with a simple layout.

Putting your headline at the top, your offer in the bottom right corner, and your pictures in the middle may not sound exciting, but it will generally bring better results.

Try to do your layout in blocks. By this I mean placing the headline, copy, pictures, and coupon in a blocked, or balanced, layout on the page. Keep it tight and don't leave too much empty space on the page. You're paying for these marketing pieces, so use every bit of them.

If you want your piece to look professional, you should pay a graphic designer to do it for you. Professional designers can be quite expensive. If you want to save some money, contact a college or university that runs a graphic design course. This way you may be able to find a second or third year student who will do it for a reasonable price. You might also consider getting a graphic artist to do just the first layout for you. Once you have this, you can then use it as a template for any future pieces.

Stock

Stock is the term used for the type of paper or card that you print your job on. There are numerous types from which to choose. Should you use glossy paper or plain paper? Plain card or a textured card? These are just some of the questions to be answered when choosing stock.

Just as there are a variety of materials from which to choose, there are also a variety of prices, ranging from the very expensive to the downright cheap. Before deciding on the type to use, you need to consider the type of product you're about to promote.

If you're selling expensive, good-quality products, you'll need to use better-quality stock than you would for a cheaper product. You need to understand that by using high-quality stock, your prospects will believe yours is a high quality product.

Printing

Another consideration in the creation of your Point of Sale System is how to have your material printed. This will depend largely on your budget, as well as the type of product you're trying to sell. You basically have three choices:

- **Professional printer:** This is more expensive but ensures that your material will look first rate. Always have your pieces professionally printed if your budget allows. This is a must for those higher-priced products.

- **Personal printer:** If you own, or have access to, a good-quality computer printer, you may be able to save on your printing costs. However, you need to keep in mind the quality of the stock you use and the price of your product. If you were printing a large number of posters or flyers, it would probably work out more cost-effectively in the long run to have them done professionally. You also need to keep in mind the size of things like store signs and posters. Because many of them will be hanging on a wall, or need to be read from a distance, you need to print them on large paper or card. The average personal printer will not be able to handle larger paper sizes.

- **Photocopies:** This is the bargain basement of printing. If you decide to go with this option, make sure the quality of reproduction is high. Having black lines all over your material will make you, and your product, look cheap. Use this option only as a last resort.

Step 5: How Big Should Your Point of Sale System Be?

I'm glad you asked. See, there is a point where you can overdo your Point of Sale System. If you have too many things for people to read and look at, they will become confused or desensitized to it, and just not pay any attention at all.

You see, the trick to having a good system is this: people need to view it as an assistance to them, not an intrusion.

If they think your project sheets and catalogues actually help them shop in your store, they'll enjoy coming to you. On the other hand, if they're being bombarded with information and have things shoved in their face every time they turn a corner, they'll feel uncomfortable and won't come back.

I've spoken about a lot of different elements that contribute towards making a successful Point of Sale System, but for the average business, I'd say using all of them would amount to overkill. You're better off simply choosing the ones you think will work best for your business, do them on a small scale to start with, and then test and measure.

You'll already have many of the elements produced and at your disposal. Things like catalogs and brochures are commonplace in most businesses, so it's simply a matter of using them more effectively. When you look at it, there's no need to spend thousands of dollars on your Point of Sale System. Because you'll already have a few of the things I've mentioned, you can afford to invest in a few of the things you don't have in place.

Understand that there's a lot more to working out the right size for a Point of Sale System than most people think. Because most of the expense you'll incur is in the printing, it's usually a case of, "How much can we afford to spend on the printing?"

The question really should be, "How much do we want to make?" If the material is good enough, it should make you money—not drain your funds.

If you don't have a marketing piece that you know works, you need to guess. You need to think about how many responses you need to break even. That means, how many sales you need to pay back the advertising cost.

Here's how you work it out:

First, you need to work out your average profit. To do this, measure the amount of profit on each sale, every day for three days. Then find the average. If you want to skip the hard work, estimate this figure.

Next, get a few quotes on the cost of printing. Remember that the idea is to keep the costs as low as possible, so get as many quotes as you can. This of course won't be such an issue if you decide to photocopy your newsletters, or run them off on your own printer.

Now, divide the production cost by your average profit. This will give you the number of sales you need to pay for the campaign.

Here's an example:

Let's say a hairdresser makes about $15 profit from each sale of shampoo and conditioner. The salon spends around $270 getting its Point of Sale material printed. That means they need 18 customers to buy shampoo and conditioner as a result of their Point of Sale System. Anything less and the system is costing the salon money.

So work out how much your system is going to cost, and how much you need to sell to cover it. With a bit of time and effort, you'll come up with the system that's right for you.

Step 6: How Often Should You Change Your Point of Sale Material?

This depends largely on the type of business you're in, and on how often your clients come in to your store.

Let me explain why.

Your Point of Sale System works well when it's new and exciting to people. Once they've seen it a few times, they become used to it and start to ignore it. So it follows that if yours is the type of business people visit once or twice a week (supermarket, hardware store, etc) then you'll need to change your system more often.

But if you own a clothing store, and your clients come in on average three to four times a year, you won't need to change it as often.

People make the mistake of thinking that because a poster has been on the wall for a month or two, people aren't noticing it. But if many of your clients haven't been to your store for three or more months, it's all new to them and will work as well as it did the first time you put it up. Understand that you'll get sick of your Point of Sale material before you clients will.

But obviously, don't leave it until it's become well and truly dated. People are going to get a bit annoyed if your project sheets haven't changed since they were in your store six months ago. Keep things fresh and rotate your material as you have to. Remember there's a lot of benefit in making changes for the sake of your team members. If things look the same to them day in and day out, they'll start to lose the passion for what they're doing.

Step 7: What Else Do You Need to Think About?

Use this section as a final checklist. Once you're happy with your Point of Sale material, run through and make sure you're ready to get started. Here are a few things you may not have thought of:

Production: Make sure you check everything before it goes to print. Ask for a "proof" (finished copy) of the publication and check it thoroughly. Don't let anything go out with spelling mistakes or the wrong offer.

Check Stock and Staff Levels: It's unlikely your new system will have your team run off their feet (very few actually do), but you need to be prepared for a sizable response. There would be nothing worse than implementing a successful Point of Sale System and then running out of stock or being too busy to service the additional enquiries it brings in. Plan for the system and make sure you can cater to any increased demand.

There's another thing I'd like to touch on—store layout:

While it's not the intention of this book to delve too deeply into this area, it is worth mentioning. Putting a bit of thought into how your store is laid out will increase the enjoyment of customers who visit you. A good example of this is a pharmacy I know that completely redid the layout of its store.

See, the pharmacy owners and employees understood that narrow aisles and tall shelves made it difficult for some of their customers to shop there. Many of the people who came to them were elderly, had walkers and couldn't negotiate the narrow corridors between the aisles. They also had difficulty in reaching items at the top of their existing shelves.

But there was another group of people who also had trouble in these areas—people in wheelchairs. Now they understood that by catering to these groups, they'd get 100 percent of that market. Best of all, they wouldn't lose any of their other customers by making a few changes. In fact, when they increased the space between the aisles and replaced the tall shelves with shorter ones, many of their younger clients also found the store to be more user friendly. Now it took a bit of time to work out how to get the same amount of stock into the store, but as a team they got together and worked out a solution. But it doesn't end there.

There was still another market nobody had catered to, whom they wanted as customers—breast-feeding mothers. It can be awkward for mothers who need to feed their babies but don't have somewhere private to do it. The shopping center they were in didn't really cater to them, as they expected them to use the center's toilets. Now as soon as the store put in a maternity room, young mothers started flocking there in droves. Some of them simply wanted to use the clean and comfortable facilities, but all of them made some purchases, albeit small ones. The store's profit went through the roof.

Now, I'm not suggesting these ideas will work for every business, but it is worth taking a moment to look at your store to see if it can be improved.

A good example of a business that did just that is a clothing store I once visited.

Now, let me explain to you the frustration of being a male in a female clothing store. If you're a man, you'll know what I mean, but for the females reading this book, let me paint the picture for you:

You're standing in a store full of women trying on clothes. There is nothing for you to look at, other than the floor. You feel uncomfortable, to say the least. It's as if every other person in the store is looking at you and thinking you're a pervert. All you want to do is get out.

So what do you do? You rush your wife or girlfriend, urging them to hurry up so you can get out of there. Now is this what you, the store owner, want? No. You want people to come in, spend as long as they like there, so you get the chance to sell them something else.

Well, this particular women's clothing store personnel realized that the longer their customers stayed in the store, the greater the chance they had of making a sale. So they invested just a few hundred dollars in comfortable armchairs, a big-screen TV, and a minibar full of light beers so the husbands and boyfriends had something to do while their partners "shopped till they dropped."

Now not only do the males prefer going there to avoid the other more embarrassing stores, they would actually try to get their partners to stay in the store longer. You see, this store had sports playing on the big screen, because they knew if men got involved in a game, they would not want to leave in a hurry. They would actually give their partners more money to spend, just so they could keep watching the game!

So try to put yourself in the shoes of the customer when you look at your store. If it is not user friendly, and makes some people feel uncomfortable, the chances are you're losing business.

"So there you are, Charlie; I've now shown you everything you need to know to generate more sales for your business. The next step involves developing a timetable for their introduction. Just how that is done and over what period will be decided at our next session. I'd like you to first spend some time digesting what you have learned today. How does that sound?"

"Great. My head is spinning, but I can certainly see real possibilities for the business. In fact, I'm really excited and can't wait to begin the next phase."

I pushed back my chair, stood up, and walked across to the window for a better look into the workshop.

"Now, about that Porsche 911 Carrera Cabriolet over there—What's it got in it?"

"You'll never believe it, man. That car. . . ."

We chatted for 20 minutes about the advantages of installing a wind deflector.

"You won't believe the difference they make," he continued. "This optional item was developed in the Porsche wind tunnel to help minimize turbulence at speed. As well as being extremely easy to install, it can be folded away neatly in the luggage compartment when not in use. I can have one here for you within a week, Brad. When would suit you best?"

"Hey, you're sounding like a seasoned salesman already. That's what I like to hear. But seriously, do you think they're worth the money?"

"Absolutely. From the feedback I get, most owners say they wouldn't be without one. Now, when did you say you'd bring your car in?"

Conclusion

So there you have it—everything you need to get your cash registers ringing.

Selling strategies serve a very important purpose in business—any business. First, they'll focus your mind on your prospects and what their needs and desires are. Second, by requiring the use of great selling techniques and skills, they'll maximize your chances of adding to your bottom line. You see, every business *needs* to sell. What good is it if you produce a great product that nobody wants?

Once you've worked your way through this book, you'll know how to write effective scripts. You'll know what it takes to produce quotes that work. You'll understand what great customer service really is and how to get your prospects to become Raving Fans. You'll also know about the power of the telephone and how you can maximize its potential to your benefit. You'll know how to harness the benefits of Point of Sale material so you can sell more to your customers.

After reading this book you'll understand how to analyze the costs involved and how to work out what your break-even point is. You'll quickly develop selling strategies that will be the envy of your competitors because you'll really understand how to test and measure every step along the way.

So what are you waiting for?

Get into *Action* now.

Getting into *Action*

So, when is the best time to start?

Now—right now—so let me give you a step-by-step method to get yourself onto the same success path of many of my clients and the clients of my team at *Action International*.

Start testing and measuring now.

You'll want to ask your customers and prospects how they found out about you and your business. This will give you an idea of what's been working and what hasn't. You also want to concentrate on the five areas of the business chassis. Remember:

1. Number of Leads from each campaign.
2. Conversion Rate from each and every campaign.
3. Number of Transactions on average per year per customer.
4. Average Dollar Sale from each campaign.
5. Your Margins on each product or service.

The Number of Leads is easy; just take a measure for four weeks, average it out, and multiply by 50 working weeks of the year. Of course you'd ask each lead where they came from so you've got enough information to make advertising decisions.

The Conversion Rate is a little trickier, not because it's hard to measure, but because we want to know a few more details. You want to know what level of conversion you have from each and every type of marketing strategy you use. Remember that some customers won't buy right away, so keep accurate records on each and every lead.

To find the Number of Transactions you'll need to go through your records. Hopefully you can find the transaction history of at least 50 of your past customers and then average out their yearly purchases.

The Average Dollar Sale is as simple as it sounds. The total dollars sold divided by the number of sales. The best information you can collect is the average from each marketing campaign you run, so that you know where the real profit is coming from.

And, of course, your margins. An Average Margin is good to know and measure, but to know the margins on everything you sell is the most powerful knowledge you can collect.

If you're having any challenges with your testing and measuring, be sure to contact your nearest *Action International* Business Coach. She'll be able to help you through and show you the specialized documents to use.

If, by chance, you're thinking of racing ahead before you test and measure, remember this. It's impossible to improve a score when you don't know what the score is.

So you've got your starting point. You know exactly what's going on in your business right now. In fact, you know more about not only what's happening right now, but also the factors that are going to create what will happen tomorrow.

The next step in your business growth is simple.

Let's decide what you want out of the business—in other words, your goals. Here are the main points I want you to plan for.

How many hours do you want to work each week? How much money do you want to take out of the business each month? And, most importantly, when do you want to finish the business?

By "finish" the business, I mean when it will be systematized enough so it can run without your having to be there. Remember this about business; a little bit of planning goes a long way, but to make a plan you have to have a destination.

Once again, if you're having difficulty, talk to an *Action International* Business Coach. He'll know exactly how to help you find what it is you really want out of both your business and your life.

Now the real work begins.

Remember, our goal is to get a 10 percent increase in each area over the next 12 months. Choose well, but I want to warn you of one thing, one thing I can literally guarantee.

Eight out of 10 marketing campaigns you run *will not work.*

That's why when you choose to run, say, an advertising campaign in your local newspaper, you've got to run at least 10 different ads. When you select a direct mail campaign, you should send out at least 10 different letters to test, and so on.

Make sure you get at least five strategies under each heading and plan to run at least one, preferably two, at least each month for the next 12 months.

Don't work on just one of the five areas at a time; mix it up a little so you get the synergy of all five areas working together.

Now, this is the most important advice I can give you:

Learn how to make each and every strategy work. Don't just think you know what to do; go through my hints and tips, read more books, listen to as many tapes as you can, watch all the videos you can find, talk to the experts, and make sure you get the most advantage you can before you invest a whole lot of money.

The next 12 months are going to be a matter of doing the numbers, running the campaigns, testing headlines, testing offers, testing prices, and, of course, measuring the results.

By the end of it you should have at least five new strategies in each of the five areas working together to produce a great result.

Once again I want to stress that this will work and this will make your business grow as long as *you* work it.

Is it simple? *Yes.*

Is it easy? *No.*

You'll have to work hard. If you can get the guidance of someone who's been there before you, then get it.

Whatever you do, start it now, start it today, and most importantly, make the most of every day. Your past does not equal your future; you decide your future right here and right now.

Be who you want to be, *do* what you need to do, in order to *have* what you want to have.

Positive *thought* without positive *Action* leaves you with positively *nothing*. I called my company **ActionCOACH** for this very reason.

So take the first step—and get into *Action*.

ABOUT THE AUTHOR

Bradley J. Sugars

Brad Sugars is a world-renowned Australian entrepreneur, author, and business coach who has helped more than a million clients around the world find business and personal success.

He's a trained accountant, but as he puts it, most of his experience comes from owning his own companies. Brad's been in business for himself since age 15 in some way or another, although his father would argue he started at 7 when he was caught selling his Christmas presents to his brothers. He's owned and operated more than two dozen companies, from pizza to ladies fashion, from real estate to insurance and many more.

His main company, **ActionCOACH,** started from humble beginnings in the back bedroom of a suburban home in 1993 when Brad started teaching business owners how to grow their sales and marketing results. Now **ActionCOACH** has over 1000 franchises in 26 countries and is ranked in the top 100 franchises in the world.

Brad Sugars has spoken on stage with the likes of Tom Hopkins, Brian Tracy, John Maxwell, Robert Kiyosaki, and Allen Pease, written books with people like Anthony Robbins, Jim Rohn, and Mark Victor Hansen, appeared on countless TV and radio programs and in literally hundreds of print articles around the globe. He's been voted as one of the Most Admired Entrepreneurs by the readers of *E-Spy* magazine—next to the likes of Rupert Murdoch, Henry Ford, Richard Branson, and Anita Roddick.

Today, **ActionCOACH** has coaches across the globe and is ranked as one of the Top 25 Fastest Growing Franchises on the planet as well as the #1 Business Consulting Franchise. The success of **ActionCOACH** is simply attributed to the fact that they apply the strategies their coaches use with business owners.

Brad is a proud father and husband, the chairman of a major children's charity, and in his own words, "a very average golfer."

Check out Brad's Web site www.bradsugars.com and read the literally hundreds of testimonials from those who've gone before you.

RECOMMENDED READING LIST

ACTION INTERNATIONAL BOOK LIST

"The only difference between *you* now and *you* in 5 years' time will be the people you meet and the books you read." Charlie Tremendous Jones

"And, the only difference between *your* income now and *your* income in 5 years' time will be the people you meet, the books you read, the tapes you listen to, and then how *you* apply it all." Brad Sugars

- *The E-Myth Revisited* by Michael E. Gerber
- *My Life in Advertising & Scientific Advertising* by Claude Hopkins
- *Tested Advertising Methods* by John Caples
- *Building the Happiness Centered Business* by Dr. Paddi Lund
- *Write Language* by Paul Dunn & Alan Pease
- *7 Habits of Highly Effective People* by Steven Covey
- *First Things First* by Steven Covey
- *Awaken the Giant Within* by Anthony Robbins
- *Unlimited Power* by Anthony Robbins
- *22 Immutable Laws of Marketing* by Al Ries & Jack Trout
- *21 Ways to Build a Referral Based Business* by Brad Sugars
- *21 Ways to Increase Your Advertising Response* by Mark Tier
- *The One Minute Salesperson* by Spencer Johnson & Larry Wilson
- *The One Minute Manager* by Spencer Johnson & Kenneth Blanchard
- *The Great Sales Book* by Jack Collis
- *Way of the Peaceful Warrior* by Dan Millman
- *How to Build a Championship Team*—Six Audio tapes by Blair Singer
- Brad Sugars "Introduction to Sales & Marketing" 3-hour Video
- Leverage—Board Game by Brad Sugars
- *17 Ways to Increase Your Business Profits* booklet & tape by Brad Sugars. FREE OF CHARGE to Business Owners

*To order Brad Sugars' products from the recommended reading list, call your nearest *Action International* office today.

The 18 Most Asked Questions about Working with an ActionCOACH Business Coach

And 18 great reasons why you'll jump at the chance to get your business flying and make your dreams come true

1. So who is ActionCOACH?

ActionCOACH is a business Coaching and Consulting company started in 1993 by entrepreneur and author Brad Sugars. With offices around the globe and business coaches from Singapore to Sydney to San Francisco, **ActionCOACH** has been set up with you, the business owner, in mind.

Unlike traditional consulting firms, **ActionCOACH** is designed to give you both short-term assistance and long-term training through its affordable Mentoring approach. After 14 years teaching business owners how to succeed, **ActionCOACH**'s more than 10,000 clients and 1,000,000 seminar attendees will attest to the power of the programs.

Based on the sales, marketing, and business management systems created by Brad Sugars, your **ActionCOACH** is trained to not only show you how to increase your business revenues and profits, but also how to develop the business so that you as the owner work less and relax more.

ActionCOACH is a franchised company, so your local **ActionCOACH** is a fellow business owner who's invested her own time, money, and energy to make her business succeed. At **ActionCOACH,** your success truly does determine our success.

2. And, why do I need a Business Coach?

Every great sports star, business person, and superstar is surrounded by coaches and advisors.

And, as the world of business moves faster and gets more competitive, it's difficult to keep up with both the changes in your industry and the innovations in sales, marketing, and management strategies. Having a business coach is no longer a luxury; it's become a necessity.

On top of all that, it's impossible to get an objective answer from yourself. Don't get me wrong. You can survive in business without the help of a Coach, but it's almost impossible to thrive.

A Coach *can* see the forest for the trees. A Coach will make you focus on the game. A Coach will make you run more laps than you feel like. A Coach will tell it like it is. A Coach will give you small pointers. A Coach will listen. A Coach will be your marketing manager, your sales director, your training coordinator, your partner, your confidant, your mentor, your best friend, and an *Action* Business Coach will help you make your dreams come true.

3. Then, what's an Alignment Consultation?

Great question. It's where an *Action* Coach starts with every business owner. You'll invest a minimum of $1295, and during the initial 2 to 3 hours your Coach invests with you, he'll learn as much as he can about your business, your goals, your challenges, your sales, your marketing, your finances, and so much more.

All with three goals in mind: To know exactly where your business is now. To clarify your goals both in the business and personally. And thirdly, to get the crucial pieces of information he needs to create your businesses *Action* Plan for the next 12 months.

Not a traditional business or marketing plan mind you, but a step-by-step plan of *Action* that you'll work through as you continue with the Mentor Program.

4. So, what, then, is the Mentor Program?

Simply put, it's where your *Action* Coach will work with you for a full 12 months to make your goals a reality. From weekly coaching calls and goal-setting sessions, to creating marketing pieces together, you will develop new sales strategies and business systems so you can work less and learn all that you need to know about how to make your dreams come true.

You'll invest between $995 and $10,000 a month and your Coach will dedicate a minimum of 5 hours a month to working with you on your sales, marketing, team building, business development, and every step of the *Action* Plan you created from your Alignment Consultation.

Unlike most consultants, your *Action* Coach will do more than just show you what to do. She'll be with you when you need her most, as each idea takes shape, as each campaign is put into place, as you need the little pointers on making it happen, when you need someone to talk to, when you're faced with challenges and, most importantly, when you're just not sure what to do next. Your Coach will be there every step of the way.

5. Why at least 12 months?

If you've been in business for more than a few weeks, you've seen at least one or two so called "quick fixes."

Most Consultants seem to think they can solve all your problems in a few hours or a few days. At *Action* we believe that long-term success means not just scraping the surface and doing it for you. It means doing it with you, showing you how to do it, working alongside you, and creating the success together.

Over the 12 months, you'll work on different areas of your business, and month by month you'll not only see your goals become a reality, you'll gain both the confidence and the knowledge to make it happen again and again, even when your first 12 months of Coaching is over.

6. How can you be sure this will work in my industry and in my business?

Very simple. You see at *Action,* we're experts in the areas of sales, marketing, business development, business management, and team building just to name a few. With 328 different profit-building strategies, you'll soon see just how powerful these systems are.

You, on the other hand, are the expert in your business and together we can apply the *Action* systems to make your business fly.

Add to this the fact that within the *Action* Team at least one of our Coaches has either worked with, managed, worked in, or even owned a business that's the same or very similar to yours. Your *Action* Coach has the full resources of the entire *Action* team to call upon for every challenge you have. Imagine hundreds of experts ready to help you.

7. Won't this just mean more work?

Of course when you set the plan with your *Action* Coach, it'll all seem like a massive amount of work, but no one ever said attaining your goals would be easy.

In the first few months, it'll take some work to adjust, some work to get over the hump so to speak. The further you are into the program, the less and less work you'll have to do.

You will, however, be literally amazed at how focused you'll be and how much you'll get done. With focus, an *Action* Coach, and most importantly the *Action* Systems, you'll be achieving a whole lot more with the same or even less work.

8. How will I find the time?

Once again the first few months will be the toughest, not because of an extra amount of work, but because of the different work. In fact, your *Action* Coach will show you how to, on a day-to-day basis, get more work done with less effort.

In other words, after the first few months you'll find that you're not working more, just working differently. Then, depending on your goals from about month six onwards, you'll start to see the results of all your work, and if you choose to, you can start working less than ever before. Just remember, it's about changing what you do with your time, *not* putting in more time.

9. How much will I need to invest?

Nothing, if you look at it from the same perspective as we do. That's the difference between a cost and an investment. Everything you do with your *Action* Coach is a true investment in your future.

Not only will you create great results in your business, but you'll end up with both an entrepreneurial education second to none, and the knowledge that you can repeat your successes over and over again.

As mentioned, you'll need to invest at least $1295 up to $5000 for the Alignment Consultation and Training Day, and then between $995 and $10,000 a month for the next 12 months of coaching.

Your Coach may also suggest several books, tapes, and videos to assist in your training, and yes, they'll add to your investment as you go. Why? Because having an *Action* Coach is just like having a marketing manager, a sales team leader, a trainer, a recruitment specialist, and corporate consultant all for half the price of a secretary.

10. Will it cost me extra to implement the strategies?

Once again, give your *Action* Coach just half an hour and he'll show you how to turn your marketing into an investment that yields sales and profits rather than just running up your expenses.

In most cases we'll actually save you money when we find the areas that aren't working for you. But yes, I'm sure you'll need to spend some money to make some money.

Yet, when you follow our simple testing and measuring systems, you'll never risk more than a few dollars on each campaign, and when we find the ones that work, we make sure you keep profiting from them time and again.

Remember, when you go the accounting way of saving costs, you can only ever add a few percent to the bottom line.

Following Brad Sugars' formula, your *Action* Coach will show you that through sales, marketing, and income growth, your possible returns are exponential.

The sky's the limit, as they say.

11. Are there any guarantees?

To put it bluntly, no. Your *Action* Coach will never promise any specific results, nor will she guarantee that any of your goals will become a reality.

You see, we're your coach. You're still the player, and it's up to you to take the field. Your Coach will push you, cajole you, help you, be there for you, and even do some things with you, but you've still got to do the work.

Only *you* can ever be truly accountable for your own success and at *Action* we know this to be a fact. We guarantee to give you the best service we can, to answer your questions promptly, and with the best available information. And, last but not least your *Action* Coach is committed to making you successful whether you like it or not.

That's right, once we've set the goals and made the plan, we'll do whatever it takes to make sure you reach for that goal and strive with all your might to achieve all that you desire.

Of course we'll be sure to keep you as balanced in your life as we can. We'll make sure you never compromise either the long-term health and success of your company or yourself, and more importantly your personal set of values and what's important to you.

12. What results have other business owners seen?

Anything from previously working 60 hours a week down to working just 10—right through to increases in revenues of 100s and even 1000s of percent. Results speak for themselves. Be sure to keep reading for specific examples of real people, with real businesses, getting real results.

There are three reasons why this will work for you in your business. Firstly, your *Action* Coach will help you get 100 percent focused on your goals and the step-by-step processes to get you there. This focus alone is amazing in its effect on you and your business results.

Secondly, your coach will hold you accountable to get things done, not just for the day-to-day running of the business, but for the dynamic growth of the business. You're investing in your success and we're going to get you there.

Thirdly, your Coach is going to teach you one-on-one as many of *Action's* 328 profit-building strategies as you need. So whether your goal is to be making more money, or working fewer hours or both inside the next 12 months your goals can become a reality. Just ask any of the thousands of existing *Action* clients, or more specifically, check out the results of 19 of our most recent clients shown later in this section.

13. What areas will you coach me in?

There are five main areas your *Action* Coach will work on with you. Of course, how much of each depends on you, your business, and your goals.

Sales. The backbone of creating a superprofitable business, and one area we'll help you get spectacular results in.

Marketing and Advertising. If you want to get a sale, you've got to get a prospect. Over the next 12 months your *Action* Coach will teach you Brad Sugars' amazingly simple streetwise marketing—marketing that makes profits.

Team Building and Recruitment. You'll never *wish* for the right people again. You'll have motivated and passionate team members when your Coach shows you how.

Systems and Business Development. Stop the business from running you and start running your business. Your Coach will show you the secrets to having the business work, even when you're not there.

Customer Service. How to deliver consistently, make it easy to buy, and leave your customers feeling delighted with your service. Both referrals and repeat business are centered in the strategies your Coach will teach you.

14. Can you also train my people?

Yes. We believe that training your people is almost as important as coaching you.

Your investment starts at $1500 for your entire team, and you can decide between five very powerful in-house training programs. From "*Sales Made Simple*" for your face-to-face sales team to "*Phone Power*" for your entire team's telephone etiquette and sales ability. Then you can run the *"Raving Fans"* customer service training or the *"Total Team"* training. And finally, if you're too busy earning a living to make any real money, then you've just got to attend our *"Business Academy 101."* It will make a huge impact on your finances, business, career, family, and lifestyle. You'll be amazed at how much involvement and excitement comes out of your team with each training program.

15. Can you write ads, letters, and marketing pieces for me?

Yes. Your *Action* Coach can do it for you, he can train you to do it yourself, or we can simply critique the marketing pieces you're using right now.

If you want us to do it for you, our one-time fees start at just $1195. You'll not only get one piece; we'll design several pieces for you to take to the market and see which one performs the best. Then, if it's a critique you're after, just $349 means we'll work through your entire piece and give you feedback on what to change, how to change it, and what else you should do. Last but not least, for between $15 and $795 we can recommend a variety of books, tapes, and most importantly, Brad Sugars' Instant Success series books that'll take you step-by-step through the how-tos of creating your marketing pieces.

16. Why do you also recommend books, tapes, and videos?

Basically, to save you time and money. Take Brad Sugars' *Sales Rich* DVD or Video Series, for instance. In about 16 hours you'll learn more about business than you have in the last 12 years. It'll also mean your *Action* Coach works with you on the high-level implementation rather than the very basic teaching.

It's a very powerful way for you to speed up the coaching process and get phenomenal rather than just great results.

17. When is the best time to get started?

Yesterday. OK, seriously, right now, today, this minute, before you take another step, waste another dollar, lose another sale, work too many more hours, miss another family event, forget another special occasion.

Far too many business people wait and see. They think working harder will make it all better. Remember, what you know got you to where you are. To get to where you want to go, you've got to make some changes and most probably learn something new.

There's no time like the present to get started on your dreams and goals.

18. So how do we get started?

Well, you'd better get back in touch with your *Action* Coach. There's some very simple paperwork to sign, and then you're on your way.

You'll have to invest a few hours showing them everything about your business. Together you'll get a plan created and then the work starts. Remember, it may seem like a big job at the start, but with a Coach, you're sharing the load and together you'll achieve great things.

Here's what others say about what happened after working with an *Action* business coach

Paul and Rosemary Rose—Icontact Multimedia

"Our *Action* coach showed us several ways to help market our product. We went on to triple our client base and simultaneously tripled our profits in just seven months. It was unbelievable! Last year was our best Christmas ever. We were really able to spoil ourselves!"

S. Ford—Pride Kitchens

"In 6 months, I've gone from working more than 60 hours per week in my business to less than 20, and my conversion rate's up from 19 percent to 62 percent. I've now got some life back!"

Gary and Leanne Paper—Galea Timber Products

"We achieved our goal for the 12 months within a 6-month period with a 100 percent increase in turnover and a good increase in margins. We have already recommended and will continue to recommend this program to others."

Russell, Kevin, John, and Karen—Northern Lights Power and Distribution

"Our profit margin has increased from 8 percent to 21 percent in the last 8 months. *Action* coaching focussed us on what are our most profitable markets."

Ty Pedersen—De Vries Marketing Sydney

"After just three months of coaching, my sales team's conversion rate has grown from an average of less than 12 percent to more than 23 percent and our profits have climbed by more than 30 percent."

Hank Meerkerk and Hemi McGarvey—B.O.P. School of Welding

"Last year we started off with a profit forecast, but as soon as we got *Action* involved we decided to double our forecast. We're already well over that forecast again by two-and-a-half times on turnover, and profits are even higher. Now we run a really profitable business."

Stuart Birch—Education Personnel Limited

"One direct mail letter added $40,000 to my bottom line, and working with *Action* has given me quality time to work on my business and spend time with my family."

Mark West—Wests Pumping and Irrigation

"In four months two simple strategies have increased our business more than 20 percent. We're so busy, we've had to delay expanding the business while we catch up!"

Michael Griffiths—Gym Owner

"I went from working 70 hours per week *in* the business to just 25 hours, with the rest of the time spent working *on* the business."

Cheryl Standring—In Harmony Landscapes

"We tried our own direct mail and only got a 1 percent response. With *Action* our response rate increased to 20 percent. It's definitely worth every dollar we've invested."

Jason and Chris Houston—Empradoor Finishing

"After 11 months of working with *Action,* we have increased our sales by 497 percent, and the team is working without our having to be there."

Michael Avery—Coomera Pet Motels

"I was skeptical at first, but I knew we needed major changes in our business. In 2 months, our extra profits were easily covering our investment and our predictions for the next 10 months are amazing."

Garry Norris—North Tax & Accounting

"As an accountant, my training enables me to help other business people make more money. It is therefore refreshing when someone else can help me do the same. I have a policy of only referring my clients to people who are professional, good at what they do, and who have personally given me great service. *Action* fits all three of these criteria, and I recommend *Action* to my business clients who want to grow and develop their businesses further."

Lisa Davis and Steve Groves—Mt. Eden Motorcycles

"With *Action* we increased our database from 800 to 1200 in 3 months. We consistently get about 20 new qualified people on our database each week for less than $10 per week."

Christine Pryor—U-Name-It Embroidery

"Sales for August this year have increased 352 percent. We're now targeting a different market and we're a lot more confident about what we're doing."

Joseph Saitta and Michelle Fisher—Banyule Electrics

"Working with *Action,* our inquiry rate has doubled. In four months our business has changed so much our customers love us. It's a better place for people to work and our margins are widening."

Kevin and Alison Snook—Property Sales

"In the 12 months previous to working with *Action,* we had sold one home in our subdivision. In the first eight months of working with *Action,* we sold six homes. The results speak for themselves."

Wayne Manson—Hospital Supplies

"When I first looked at the Mentoring Program it looked expensive, but from the inside looking out, its been the best money I have ever spent. Sales are up more than $3000 per month since I started, and the things I have learned and expect to learn will ensure that I will enjoy strong sustainable growth in the future."

▌ *Action* Contact Details

Action International **Asia Pacific**

Ground Floor, *Action* House, 2 Mayneview Street, Milton QLD 4064

Ph: +61 (0) 7 3368 2525

Fax: +61 (0) 7 3368 2535

Free Call: 1800 670 335

Action International **Europe**

Olympic House, Harbor Road, Howth, Co. Dublin, Ireland

Ph: +353 (0) 1-832 0213

Fax: +353 (0) 1-839 4934

Action International **North America**

5670 Wynn Road Suite A & C, Las Vegas, Nevada 89118

Ph: +1 (702) 795 3188

Fax: +1 (702) 795 3183

Free Call: (888) 483 2828

Action International **UK**

3-5 Richmond Hill, Richmond, Surrey TW106RE

Ph: +44 020 8948 5151

Fax: +44 020 8948 4111

Action Offices around the globe:

Australia | Canada | China | England | France | Germany | Hong Kong

India | Indonesia | Ireland | Malaysia | Mexico | New Zealand

Phillippines | Scotland | Spain | Singapore | USA | Wales

Here's how you can profit from all of Brad's ideas with your local
Action International **Business Coach**

Just like a sporting coach pushes an athlete to achieve optimum performance, provides them with support when they are exhausted, and teaches the athlete to execute plays that the competition does not anticipate.

A business coach will make you run more laps than you feel like. A business coach will show it like it is. And a business coach will listen.

The role of an *Action* Business Coach is to show you how to improve your business through guidance, support, and encouragement. Your coach will help you with your sales, marketing, management, team building, and so much more. Just like a sporting coach, your *Action* Business Coach will help you and your business perform at levels you never thought possible.

Whether you've been in business for a week or 20 years, it's the right time to meet with and see how you'll profit from an *Action* Coach.

As the owner of a business it's hard enough to keep pace with all the changes and innovations going on in your industry, let alone to find the time to devote to sales, marketing, systems, planning and team management, and then to run your business as well.

As the world of business moves faster and becomes more competitive, having a Business Coach is no longer a luxury; it has become a necessity. Based on the sales, marketing, and business management systems created by Brad Sugars, your *Action* Coach is trained to not only show you how to increase your business revenues and profits but also how to develop your business so that you, as the owner, can take back control. All with the aim of your working less and relaxing more. Making money is one thing; having the time to enjoy it is another.

Your *Action* Business Coach will become your marketing manager, your sales director, your training coordinator, your confidant, your mentor. In short, your *Action* Coach will help you make your business dreams come true.

ATTENTION BUSINESS OWNERS
You can increase your profits now

Here's how you can have one of Brad's *Action* International Business Coaches guide you to success.

Like every successful sporting icon or team, a business needs a coach to help it achieve its full potential. In order to guarantee your business success, you can have one of Brad's team as your business coach. You will learn about how you can get amazing results with the help of the team at *Action* International.

The business coaches are ready to take you and your business on a journey that will reward you for the rest of your life. You see, we believe *Action* speaks louder than words.

Complete and post this card to your local *Action* office to discover how our team can help you increase your income today!

Action International

The World's Number-1 Business Coaching Team

Name ....

Position ....

Company ....

Address ....

....

Country ....

Phone ....

Fax ....

Email ....

Referred by ....

How do I become an ActionCOACH Business Coach?

If you choose to invest your time and money in a great business and you're looking for a white-collar franchise opportunity to build yourself a lifestyle, an income, a way to take control of your life and, a way to get great personal satisfaction …

Then you've just found the world's best team!

Now, it's about finding out if you've got what it takes to really enjoy and thrive in this amazing business opportunity.

Here are the 4 things we look for in every ActionCOACH:

1. You've got to love succeeding

We're looking for people who love success, who love getting out there and making things happen. People who enjoy mixing with other people, people who thrive on learning and growing, and people who want to charge an hourly rate most professionals only dream of.

2. You've got to love being in charge of your own life

When you're ready to take control, the key is to be in business for yourself, but not by yourself. **ActionCOACH**'s support, our training, our world leading systems, and the backup of a global team are all waiting to give you the best chance of being an amazing business success.

3. You've got to love helping people

Being a great Coach is all about helping yourself by helping others. The first time clients thank you for showing them step by step how to make more money and work less within their business, will be the day you realize just how great being an **ActionCOACH** Business Coach really is.

4. You've got to love a great lifestyle

Working from home, setting your own timetable, spending time with family and friends, knowing that the hard work you do is for your own company and, not having to climb a so-called corporate ladder. This is what lifestyle is all about. Remember, business is supposed to give you a life, not take it away.

Our business is booming and we're seriously looking for people ready to find out more about how becoming a member of the **ActionCOACH** Business Coaching team is going to be the best decision you've ever made.

Apply online now at www.actioncoach.com

Here's how you can network, get new leads, build yourself an instant sales team, learn, grow and build a great team of supportive business owners around you by checking into your local *Action* Profit Club

Joining your local *Action* Profit Club is about more than just networking, it's also the learning and exchanging of profitable ideas.

Embark on a journey to a more profitable enterprise by meeting with fellow, like-minded business owners.

An *Action* Profit Club is an excellent way to network with business people and business owners. You will meet every two weeks for breakfast to network and learn profitable strategies to grow your business.

Here are three reasons why *Action* International's Profit Clubs work where other networking groups don't:

1. You know networking is a great idea. The challenge is finding the time and maintaining the motivation to keep it up and make it a part of your business. If you're not really having fun and getting the benefits, you'll find it gets easier to find excuses that stop you going. So, we guarantee you will always have fun and learn a lot from your bi-weekly group meetings.
2. The real problem is that so few people do any work 'on' their business. Instead they generally work "in" it, until it's too late. By being a member of an *Action* Profit Club, you get to attend FREE business-building workshops run by Business Coaches that teach you how to work "on" your business and avoid this common pitfall and help you to grow your business.
3. Unlike other groups, we have marketing systems to assist in your groups' growth rather than just relying on you to bring in new members. This way you can concentrate on YOUR business rather than on ours.

Latest statistics show that the average person knows at least 200 other contacts. By being a member of your local *Action* Profit Club, you have an instant network of around 3,000 people

Join your local *Action* Profit Club today.

Apply online now at www.actionprofitclub.com

LEVERAGE—The Game of Business
Your Business Success is just a Few Games Away

Leverage—The Game of Business is a fun way to
learn how to succeed in business fast.

**The rewards start flowing the moment you start
playing!**

Leverage is three hours of fun, learning, and
discovering how you can be an amazingly successful
business person.

It's a breakthrough in education that will have you
racking up the profits in no time. The principles you
take away from playing this game will set you up for a life of business success. It will open your
mind to what's truly possible. Apply what you learn and **sit back and watch your profits soar.**

By playing this fun and interactive business game, you will learn:

- How to quickly raise your business income
- How business people can become rich and successful in a short space of time
- How to create a business that works without you

Isn't it time you had the edge over your competition?

Leverage has been played by all age groups from 12-85 and has been a huge learning
experience for all. The most common comment we hear is: 'I thought I knew a lot, and just by
playing a simple board game I have realized I have a long way to go. The knowledge I've gained
from playing Leverage will make me thousands! Thanks for the lesson.'

To order your copy online today, please visit www.bradsugars.com

Also available in the

THE BUSINESS COACH

Learn how to master the six steps on
the ladder of success

(0-07-146672-X)

INSTANT REPEAT BUSINESS

Build a solid and loyal
customer base

(0-07-146666-5)

THE REAL ESTATE COACH

Invest in real estate with
little or no cash

(0-07-146662-2)

INSTANT SALES

Master the crucial first minute of
any sales call

(0-07-146664-9)

INSTANT PROMOTIONS

Create powerful press releases, amazing
ads, and brilliant brochures

(0-07-146665-7)

INSTANT SUCCESS

Real Results. Right Now.

Instant Success series.

INSTANT CASHFLOW

Turn every lead into a sale

(0-07-146659-2)

BILLIONAIRE IN TRAINING

Learn the wealth building secrets
of billionaires

(0-07-146661-4)

INSTANT PROFIT

Boost your bottom line with
a cash-building plan

(0-07-146668-1)

SUCCESSFUL FRANCHISING

Learn how to buy or sell a franchise

(0-07-146671-1)

INSTANT ADVERTISING

Create ads that stand out and sell

(0-07-146660-6)

INSTANT REFERRALS

Never cold call or chase after
customers again

(0-07-146667-3)

INSTANT LEADS

Generate a steady flow of leads

(0-07-146663-0)

INSTANT SYSTEMS

Stop running your business and start
growing it

(0-07-146670-3)

INSTANT TEAM BUILDING

Learn the six keys to a winning team

(0-07-146669-X)

*Your source for the strategies, skills,
and confidence every business owner
needs to succeed.*